NORTH KENT WALKS

Christine Baldwin

S.B. Publications

First published in 2010 by S. B. Publications
Tel: 01323 893498
Email: sbpublications@tiscali.co.uk

Little Hiker Series

Previous Titles
Walks in Ashdown Forest
Walks Around the Coastline of Kent
East Kent Walks (Canterbury and Ashford)
Kent Family Walks

ISBN 978-185770-3474

Designed and Typeset by EH Graphics (01273) 515527

Front cover photo: *Views at Lullingstone.*
Back cover photo: *Kit's Coty House (Ancient Stones Walk).*
Title page photo: *View across the Downs (White Horse Walk).*

Photographs by Christine Baldwin and Rita Keatley

SHORT HISTORY OF THE AREA

Kent has a rich and varied history with the earliest settlers walking here from Europe. Once the sea had carved through the chalk to create the English Channel many visitors, like the Celts, Romans and Saxons, came and left their mark. North Kent has its own special niche, where historical sites and areas of exceptional beauty are brought together with the North Downs dominating many walks, the remoteness of The Isle of Grain, reserves where nature and wildlife come together. The North Downs form the backbone across Surrey and Kent rising no higher than 650 feet. Originally dense woods of Ash, Beech, Yew and Hornbeam would have covered all but the steepest slope.

In the Middle Ages the woods were cleared and the marshes drained for sheep grazing. Today the woods have been replanted and the remaining grassland and thin chalky soils have allowed a botanical wonderland to emerge, including many rarer orchids like the Lady Orchid (only found on the North Downs in woods or scrubland) yellow Trefoils, Rock-roses and Hawkbits along with Scabious and Knapweed. Many types of butterflies are attracted to the area by the short turf and sunshine including the Adonis, Chalkhill and Common Blue. Away from the North Downs the Isle of Grain has marshland which dominates the landscape bordering the Thames allowing many species of bird and wildlife to thrive around this area along with the largest heron colony in England.

History plays its part in the area with a thirteenth century church having the graveyard mentioned in Great Expectations by Charles Dickens. Also a thirteenth century castle built to protect the local village and a fort built in 1860 which is still a dominating feature on the Thames Estuary with its torpedo channels, ready for use in the Second World War, still visible. A Pre-Roman Iron Age fort dating from 100-50 BC dominates one walk, while the Neolithic Coldrum Stones are the visible reminder of prehistoric life in the area. Staying on the Downs, ancient and modern history are recorded with a Long Barrow burial site of around 2000 BC and in the opposite direction a nature reserve to wonder at with new technology mixed with ancient Barrows. A meander through another area visits both a Bronze Age barrow, ancient woodland and a Second World War remnant.

Rambles and scrambles through picturesque reserves, a waterside delight, and visiting the area of a fourteenth century church and twelfth century house and tower will give endless hours of fun and enjoyment. Add to these walks an island with its own historical background and you will find Kent has something for everyone.

Map of Complete Walking Area

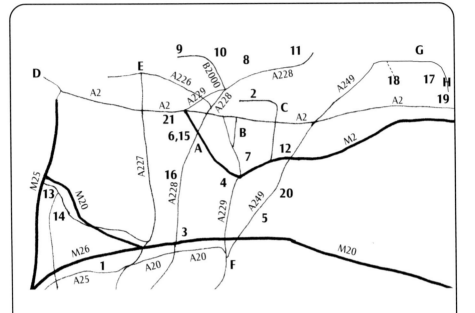

Walks Starting Point
1 Oldbury Hill Revival
2 Riverside Wonderland
3 Beauty within the Jungle
4 A Sliver of the North Downs Explored
5 The White Horse Experience
6 Cuxton's Secret Garden
7 Darland Banks Scramble
8 Northward Hill Uncovered
9 Cliffe Marshes Phenomenon
10 Cooling's Classic Encounter
11 St Mary's Magnitude
12 Queendown Warren Saunter
13 Old and Bold Explored
14 Hilltop Rise Walk
15 Ranscombe Reserve
16 Segment of the Downs Divulged

17 Harty Church, Isle of Sheppey
18 Elmley Nature Reserve, Isle of Sheppey
19 Shellness Adventure
20 Hucking Heritage (Near Maidstone)
21 A Playground for All (Jeskyns Farm)

Towns
A Rochester
B Chatham
C Gillingham
D Dartford
E Gravesend
F Maidstone
G Eastchurch (Sheppey)
H Leysdown-on-Sea (Sheppey)

Oldbury Hill Revival (Ightham)

Oldbury Hill covers 166 acres of acid greensand soil where Oak, Birch, Beech and Scots Pine dominate the landscape. The first settlements on Oldbury Camp were shelters in caves established by the Palaeolithic hunters, nearly 2,000 years ago. Towards the end of the Iron Age a hillfort was constructed with massive ramparts two and a half miles long enclosing an area of 124 acres making it one of the largest hill-forts in England. Utilized by the people living in the area as a refuge for themselves and livestock, it became an important trading post, extending the area to over 150 acres; the area was heavily defended against the Romans but proved to be no protection from the massive legions. After the Romans left the area was completely abandoned for nature to sculpture. The woods, which have been coppiced since Saxon times, are still coppiced every five to thirty years to maintain nature conservation.

On the long walk sections of the boundary wall are visible both on The Toll and along the east section heading towards the site of the south gate of the original camp, along with a spring-fed pond which attracts both wildlife and insects. The short walk encompasses the west wall, with the path passing an old defensive ditch between the inner and outer ramparts of the camp. A Prehistoric trackway creates a short cut on the long walk, while the cobbled trackway for walking and horses was once the main road in the Middle Ages (Wagon-road). On the east side of the hill rock shelters have produced evidence of occupation with finds from Palaeolithic hunters.

Oldbury Hill, pond at top of hill.

Oldbury Hill Revival (Ightham)

S   Start of Walk
■   Car Park
A   Oldbury Wood
B   Styants Wood
≈≈≈≈ Prehistoric path
⫫⫫⫫ Boundary of Oldbury Camp
- -→ Short walk
→   Long walk
=   Steps in path

1   Below western ramparts of Oldbury camp
2   Northern tip of Oldbury camp
3   Flat hilltop area forming interior of hillfort
4   Spring fed pond
5   Southern entrance to Oldbury camp
6   Old defensive ditch between inner and outer ramparts of camp
7   Eastern boundary of Oldbury camp

Access/parking:	From the M20 turn onto the A227 then onto the A25. Pass through Oldbury village then go downhill and turn off right to Oldbury Camp. Free car park on left.

Map reference: OS Explorer 147. GR578560

Distance: Short walk 1 mile. Long walk 3 miles.

Time: Short walk 35-50 minutes. Long walk 1½- 2 hours.

Terrain: Short walk: mud paths, steep climb, steep steps down.
Long walk: mud paths, steep climb, steep steps down, going round the Toll (section of north boundary of Oldbury camp)paths may be slippery.

Refreshments: Picnic benches near car park. Campsite ½ mile from car park. Crown Point Public House on A25.

Route Directions

SHORT WALK from the car park walk down the slope to the road crossing over into a clearing. Turn left walking along the mud path through Oak, Birch and Scots Pine trees looking up into woodland and catching snippets of the boundary walls of the camp. Continue along the path going down a short slope to a description board in a clearing. From here turn right walking uphill through the trees using the roots as steps, staying on the path as it bears left then right reaching the flat top just above the boundary wall which forms the interior of the hillfort. Turn right walking along a mud path passing an ancient ditch and at the junction turn right going down a short distance onto a wide flat mud leaf-covered path and turn left. Continue along to a post, which indicates the start of the steps weaving down the hill through the tree line and onto a flat mud path. Stay on the path reaching the clearing, cross over the road and up the slope to the car park.

LONG WALK From the car park walk over to the board and turn left going up the steps by the board heading into woods of Chestnut and Oak. Continue climbing up, bearing right with the path to the top of the ridge onto a wide mud path weaving through the dense Styants Wood. Stay on the path as it bears right going downhill with scant views of the campsite through the tree line. Cross over the road and bear left along the path going down the small slope to the description board in a clearing. From here continue straight on through a thin corridor of trees to the cobbled road. Turn right going uphill on the Wagon-road and turn left on the bend climbing up steps then going down steps onto a thin mud path going around The Toll, walking below a section of the ramparts as the path meanders past fallen trees on the slopes above. Continue on the path as it passes open fields on the left, then bearing right it starts to climb up going over fallen tree stumps creating log steps in the path. Stay on the path as it winds and climbs up

Section of path on long walk.

onto the top of the rampart. Once on the flat the path meets up with the Wagon-road where turn left going uphill passing many Holly trees, with Birch and Oak. The pond then comes into view on the right; carry on uphill to the junction. **(Short Cut)** Turn right onto the prehistoric road (cobbled) walking along an avenue of majestic trees as it slowly climbs. Ignore the first right fork, turning down the second fork, on a grass mud path to the end. Turn left walking along the ridge path to a post. (Go down the steps through the tree line as short walk).

(Long walk) Bear left going uphill through a corridor of Holly on a thin mud path to a junction where turn right onto a wide mud/concrete path going through dense trees. Stay on the path as it meanders through the woods following the contour of the eastern boundary of Oldbury camp and descending to the site of the southern gate.

At the junction in the dip turn right going up steps heading into woods on a mud/concrete leaf-littered path, walking around the south-western section of the boundary. Stay on the path to a post (go down the steps through the tree line as short walk).

Riverside Wonderland (Gillingham)

The Medway estuary's history goes back to Roman times as evidence shows when salt and pottery were manufactured and for four hundred years navy warships were built and docked here. This area of country park covers 100 hectares of land alongside the Medway estuary with a variety of habitats including mudflats and salt-marsh areas as well as ponds, reedbeds, grassland and scrub which all add to the diversity of the area. The estuary has been designated a Site of Special Scientific Interest and is nationally an important area for wintering birds which thrive on the rich mudflats and the specialised ecology of the saltmarsh which acts as a high tide roost site.

Areas of interest within the park are as diverse as the nature found within. Horrid Hill was once an island with the causeway being built over 100 years ago to transport materials to the cement factory that once stood at the end and a small horse-drawn railway took wagons of chalk out to the works. Historically, Horrid Hill was known as a mooring site for French prisoners during the Napoleonic Wars.

A section of the Saxon Shore path continues through the park passing Bloors wharf, which was a staging post for fishermen going out to sea but is now a scrap yard, and continues on past Rainham Dock which is now derelict but was once a thriving cement works which closed in the 1930s. The Motney Hill section of the park has an extensive area of mudflats, salt-marsh and shingle with an area around the brow designated as a RSPB reserve which attracts wading birds and wildfowl in winter. Each season brings beauty to the park; in spring the paths are lined with white blossom of the Blackthorn and Hawthorn; Reed and Sedge Warblers congregate with many other birds. Summer has the Swallow and butterflies like the small Tortoiseshell Peacock and Painted lady, which are encouraged by the wild flowers. In high summer purple Sea Lavender carpets the salt-marsh areas with the rare yellow Golden Samphire skirting the edges. Autumn brings its own diverse beauty with trees like the Elder and Rowan turning colour and the wild rose producing berries. This leads into a winter spectacle with birds like the Redshank, Grey Plover, Brent Geese and Shelduck being seen on the estuary, especially between low and high tide where they feed on tiny crabs, shellfish and shrimps. Inland Redwings and Fieldfares can be seen feeding on the berries and in the grass areas together with our very own finches.

Berengrave Reserve: This reserve was an old chalk pit, created by microscopic marine plants and animals that died and settled at the bottom of shallow warm seas, as the whole area was at one time covered by the sea. Other fossils have been found like the Echinoids (Sea Urchins) and Ammonites (Sea Snails). Flints are believed to be crystallised Sea Sponges. The area was producing chalk limestone from 1901 to 1931. At the start the chalk was shipped from Rainham Dock to local cement works. In 1912 Motney Hill opened a cement works that used the chalk literally across the road. The chalk was taken by light railway to the Wash Mills where the flint and other impurities were removed. The flint was then transported for use in the construction of roads and pottery making. The cement was produced for the rapid expansion of London and the re-building of San Francisco after the earthquake in 1906. After 1931 the area was left barren and nature took over. In 1984 the pit was designated a reserve and has slowly revived to the magnificent spectacle seen now. Boardwalks guide you through the deep wetlands and the ancient chalk areas. The hollow at the bottom of the pit, when filled with water, forms the 'lake'. The lake and reed beds are managed to provide breeding habitats for the Coot, Kingfisher, Moorhen, and Grey Heron, with Ducks and Little Grebe also living on the lake. In the more open parts of the woodland, wildflowers like the rare Round-leaved Wintergreen and the Common Spotted Orchid flourish in amongst the Sweet Chestnut, Lime, Sycamore and Hornbeam.

Lake at the bottom of the Reserve.

Remnants of chalk going down step.

Boardwalk path going into wetlands.

Riverside Wonderland (Gillingham)

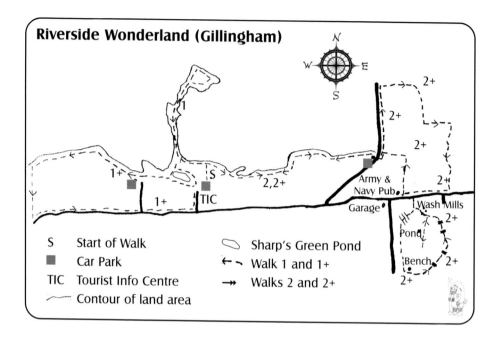

S	Start of Walk		Sharp's Green Pond
■	Car Park	← ~	Walk 1 and 1+
TIC	Tourist Info Centre	→→	Walks 2 and 2+
⌒	Contour of land area		

Access/parking: From the A2 follow A289 towards the Medway Tunnel, go straight over the first roundabout to next roundabout. Bear right along B2004 for about 1 mile; take the 1st turning left after Sharp's Green road. Free parking.

Map reference: OS Explorer 163: GR808683

Distance: Walk 1. 1¹/₂ miles, Walk 1+ = 3 miles.
Walk 2. 1³/₄ miles, Walk 2+ = 5 miles.

Time: Walk 1. ³/₄ hour, Walk 1+ = 1¹/₂ hours.
Walk 2. 50 minutes, Walk 2+ = 2¹/₂ hours.

Terrain: All the walks are on flat concrete paths with more uneven surfaces around the top of Horrid Hill.Berengrave Reserve, mud paths, boardwalks, steps.

Refreshments: Toilets in the visitor centre. Cafe sells hot and cold food. Gillingham town 2 miles.

Information: Benches are situated all along the main path. Walks can start from the car park at the end of Sharp's Green road (see map). To the right of the visitor centre go through the gate and turn left at the first junction to start the walks on flat ground out onto the estuary path.

Route Directions

WALK 1 From the car park follow the concrete path as it slowly climbs giving a breathtaking view across the estuary from the top. Go down the slope and onto the flat then turn left staying on the path as it bears right heading out into the estuary. Continue along the concrete path to a junction where bear left. This path continues round the top of Horrid Hill with benches strategically placed to give excellent views of the estuary marshes and beyond. The Kingsnorth power station looms on the horizon and over to the right, Thames port cranes and the Grain power station stand idly, giving contrasting views of the mouth of the River Medway. (There is an uneven grass path which cuts across the top of the hill walking through bushes of deadly nightshade and rosehip and coming round to the edge of the beach).

After absorbing the spectacle continue round the top returning on the same path back. Bear right at the junction and then bear left coming to the entrance of the boardwalk path (steps going down). Alternative route: continue along the concrete path and bear left at the junction then left again going down the boardwalk path on a flat surface and return on the same path which crosses over Sharp's Green pond. Coming out of the pond area turn left to return to the car park or turn right for an extra 1 hour extravaganza.

WALK 1+ Continue along the path walking beside the small inlet (Sharp's Green Bay) passing a car park (Sharp's Green road) and on past boats moored in the inlet. As the path winds continue on following the contour of the bay where benches give excellent views across the estuary. Continue on to a low wall and fence then bear left walking beside the meadow on a concrete path. Coming close to houses head down the wide alleyway out onto the main road and turn left beside the meadow. The path climbs

Reed-beds on long walk.

slowly up onto the flat; cross the road (Sharp's Green road) and at the next junction turn left into the entrance to the country park.

WALK 2 From the Tourist Information site car park either go up the concrete slope or follow the path round to Sharp's Green pond. Once on the main path (section of Saxon Shore path) bear right and follow the main concrete path as it meanders alongside the estuary. Pass through a fixed kissing gate. Going through a block of three mounds the concrete path winds through Apple trees and Deadly Nightshade before reaching the derelict Bloors wharf. Cross the wharf and bear left with the path as it goes through a corridor of Hawthorn trees and bramble bushes coming out into the open at the corner of Rainham dock. Over to the right notice a small car park. (2+start). Return by the same path back to the car park. At the junction bear round with the path heading for Horrid Hill as walk 1.

WALK 2+ Continue round, bearing left following the sea wall walking along the top on a grass path then bear right going onto the road and up the hill passing houses on the left. At the sewage works bear right going over a stile onto a mud/grass path walking around a field, down through a shaded copse then over a bridge, up some steps and, bearing right with the path, come onto a grass path which on a low level gives splendid views into the reed beds. A higher path follows the contour of the seawall alongside Otterham Creek. Coming to the corner bear left passing an orchard and continue along the path bearing round to the right passing derelict buildings onto the road. Cross over and turn right walking along the pavement heading for a pub called Small Glasses. 20 yards along at the roundabout, bear right walking along the road going straight over

Entrance out of Berengrave Nature Reserve.

another roundabout and then over a bridge; continue on, seeing a garage ahead with the Army & Navy pub on the right. 500 yards before the pub turn left into Berengrave Nature Reserve. Go straight on down the slope to a play/picnic area. Turn right going uphill on a mud path, heading into woods. Climb up the steps and once on the flat clamber over roots in the mud path, before climbing up more steps. The path is now running parallel with Berengrave Lane. Pass a pumping station on the right, walking on a mud path through woods with the road over to the right and looking down into the depth of the old chalk pit on the left. Turn left at the corner and continue along the uneven mud path. The path bears round to the left coming to steps that lead down onto a boardwalk towards the bottom of the pit. Go along and up the steps opposite, back into the woods stepping over tree roots in the mud path. As the path winds round to wooden railings the path again turns into a boardwalk going over the marsh area. Go up the next set of steps onto the top of the pit and stay on the mud path as it winds through the woods to another set of steps. Go down, bear left, ignore the path off to the right, turn left at the junction to a board on the right of the path, which is the start of the path to the lake.

Heading into the trees, the top of the lake is visible over to the right. Follow the intermittent path over fallen tree stumps, round coppiced trees down to the magnificent reed beds and open water. This area attracts birds like Kingfishers, Coot, Moorhen and ducks. Return by the same path back up through the maze of tree stumps onto the mud path and go straight on 200 yards to The Wash Mills. (Wash mills were the first stage of the processing of chalk for making cement, taking out the impurities.) Continue on to the picnic area on the right; go straight on up the slope, through the kissing gate, to the road. Turn right, go along 20 yards then cross over and go through the fixed kissing gate back into woods, walking on a concrete path to a bend. Bear right onto a grass path going up a slight slope passing Wild Rose bushes. Go through the gap onto a small heath where the yellow Biting Stonecrop mingles in with deep green ferns, daisies and other wild flowers. Over to the right a wooden fence covers a bench and viewing spot into a section of the Motney reed beds. Back on the path head through the gap on the right passing Wild Rose bushes, out through a gate and onto the road; turn left walking back along the road to the corner of Rainham Dock. At the corner bear right going round on the concrete path passing the wharf back through the gates along the concrete path where bear left back to the car park.

Wash Mills area. Stones left where mill stood.

Wetlands area.

Wetlands area.

Beauty within the Jungle (Snodland)

Leybourne Lake has evolved from a misused and abandoned building site. Opened in 2004, windsurfing, canoeing, fishing and scuba-diving blend with recreation and wildlife. The combination has opened up an area of excellence surrounded by a concrete jungle of warehouses, businesses and housing. Over 200 acres of land where six lakes are fishing areas and the main lake caters for canoeing, scuba-diving and windsurfing whilst hosting a great many wild swans, ducks, geese and other water birds.

It is now a key conservation area, protected by fencing, of small lakes and reed beds and attracts wild birds and insects while water voles are being encouraged to thrive.

Main lake.

Beauty within the Jungle (Snodland)

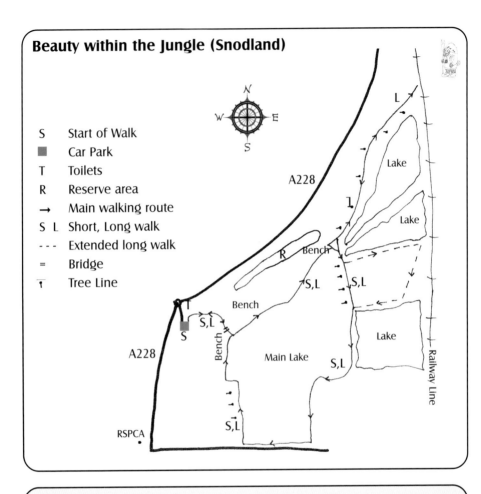

S   Start of Walk
■   Car Park
T   Toilets
R   Reserve area
→   Main walking route
S L   Short, Long walk
- - -   Extended long walk
=   Bridge
ᴛ   Tree Line

Access/parking: From the M20 take the A228 towards Rochester. At the 2nd roundabout take the third right turning into an open gateway, over speed humps into a car park. Parking - 50p 4 hours, £1 all day.

Map Reference: OS Explorer 148. GR697605

Distance: Short walk 1¹/₂ miles. Long Walk 2¹/₂+ miles

Time: Short walk 45-60 minutes. Long walk 90-120 minutes.

Terrain: Flat concrete paths. Long walk, grass paths.

Refreshments: Kiosk selling hot snacks, cold drinks on start of walk. Toilets in car park. Garage ¹/₄ mile by roundabout.

Route Directions

SHORT WALK - LONG WALK, from the car park head towards the main building. Over to the left of the building start off along the concrete path bearing right heading into trees; stay on the path as it winds round to a junction. 20 yards on bear right going over the bridge, then turn left onto a wide concrete path with the main lake on the right. Stay on the main path to a triangle junction; go directly left and left again onto a concrete/mud path passing a fenced conservation area over to the left. (Turn left on a grass path going over a small bridge towards a fence. (**SHORT WALK** bear right)

LONG WALK Back on the path continue on, passing the start of another lake on the right which is shrouded by more trees and small islands within the lake, and where fishing is permitted. On the left a small river runs beside the path, continue along as it winds round with the river. Stay on the path as it bears round to the right with a railway line to your right. Go on as far as the gate and return by the same path along the banks of the lake. At the triangle junction bear left passing a car park on the left. (EXTENDED WALK turn left walking beside the car park along the concrete path heading into grassland. Staying on the path ignore the junction on the right, go on to the end of the path, then turn right walking across the grass in a diagonal direction to the edge of a lake. Turn right walking along the edge of the lake to the junction where turn left). Long Walk **(SHORT WALK continues)** The path now passes between the main lakes. Stay on the path at it comes to a junction, turn right heading round a bend to a housing estate on the left. At a T-junction by the estate go straight onto a concrete path passing a wall on the left, with trees on the right shrouding the lake. As the path winds round, the path follows the contour of a main road on the left with the lake still visible through the trees and bushes. Bear right with the path at the junction, going round the pond and seeing the wide path over to the far right, first started out on. Coming to the corner bear slightly to the left going back over the bridge then turn left heading back through the corridor of trees on a concrete path, bearing left back into the car park.

Little island on lake.

A Sliver of the North Downs Explored

The North Downs has had a varied history starting out as dense woodland of mainly Ash, Hornbeam, Beech and Yew with the rivers Stour, Medway and Darent creating wet marshy flat areas between the scarps. Early settlements created open grazing spaces for sheep with much of the woodland cleared and the marshland drained. Much of the scarps have been replanted with trees, fields of crops and grassland dominate the landscape. The latest change is the building of the Channel Tunnel rail link, which cuts through the landscape but has left much of the original woodland in place, and where changes have been made, new planting of trees has encouraged wildlife and plants to flourish. Both walks start from Bluebell Hill; at 175 metres it forms part of the chalk downland with unforgettable views over the Medway valley. The area is classified a Site of Special Scientific Interest where rare plants thrive in the chalk land like the Bulbous Buttercup, Salad Burnet, Hairy Violet and Bee Orchid which attract insects like the Dingy and Grizzled Skipper butterfly along with the Chalkhill Blue and Brown Angus.

One walk heads down a steep slope through dense woodland of Ash and Yew and heading back through open fields and a nature reserve. Pass an isolated stone on a section of the path called The White Horse Stone (it appears that it was heading for the site of Kit's Coty but for some reason was abandoned) before coming to an ancient sarsen site on top of a slope, Kit's Coty House, which is the remains of a Long Barrow burial mound from around 2000 B.C.; this represents the early burial places of the religious leaders who were becoming more settled.

The second walk heads in the opposite direction where the path weaves through Burham Down Nature Reserve, an important area of downland, rich in wildlife; Skylarks and Kestrels are just a few of the birds seen on the downland. On through Ash, Beech and then Yew woods before coming out beside a section of the London stretch of the Channel Tunnel Rail Link. Evidence of rejuvenation is a pleasant sight as the path heads back up on a slow continual climb passing Shoulder Of Mutton Wood, its name coming from the shape of the woods forming a landmark, made up of Beech trees standing since 1600 A.D. with an ancient monument (Bell Barrow, a funerary monument dating back to the early and middle Bronze Age 1500-1200 B.C.) with a central hollow which suggests that it may have been excavated. This walk goes through more woodland, passing the top of Burham Down Nature Reserve.

Burham Down.

A Sliver of the North Downs (Ancient Stones)

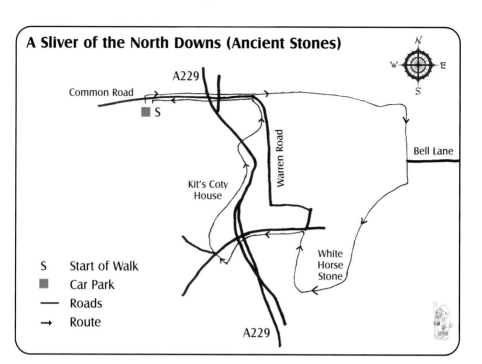

S   Start of Walk
■   Car Park
—   Roads
→   Route

Access/parking: From the M2 turn off onto the A229 towards Maidstone. Follow the sign to Bluebell Hill going along Common Road and turn left into car park. Free parking.

Map reference: OS Explorer 148. GR743621

Distance: 5¹/₂ miles

Time: 3-4 hours depending on stops

Terrain: Stiles, gates, mud paths (deep canopy paths can be wet in summer) steep downhill, steep climb, road walking.

Refreshments: No toilets in car park. Lower Bell Pub on route. Home cooked food. Open all day Monday to Saturday, Sunday 12-3pm. 6pm-10.30pm.

Route Directions

WALK 1 Ancient Stones From the car park walk out onto the road and turn right. Walk along Common Road crossing the bridge and straight over passing the Upper Bell Inn (closed down) onto Mill Lane. Continue along road to a bend where Warren Road starts, bear left towards 2 stiles. Bear right going over the stile, passing stables over to the right. Staying on the mud path walk through a canopy of trees to another stile. Climb over and stay on the path to another stile; go over and continue straight on through the woods. As the path climbs bear left at the tree root and carry straight on out of the woods by a fence. Continue on 20 yards then bear left passing Chestnut trees and head through a small wood, out into the open again. With the road on the left walk past newly-planted trees seeing radio masts ahead. Continue along the path as it climbs and turn right at the corner by the radio station. Walk along the path passing a house on the left and then bear right walking along the road between fields of crops. Coming to Bell Lane cross over the road through the gate into the field and 50 yards in bear left with the path heading across the fields with the woods on the right. Just before the farm turn right heading towards the woods. Turn right and follow the path round the edge of the woods to the opposite corner of the field. Turn left heading into the woods on a canopied path of Ash and Ivy clad trees, heading down on a steep path into a Yew wood with tree roots in the path. Still going down, the path comes out to an Ash and Willow junction. Turn right heading downhill with steps of wood in the path to aid the descent going through more Yew woods. Coming to a gate go through and turn left on to a concrete path (section of North Downs Way) heading downhill. 50 yards along look for steps on the right, which lead up to the sarsen stone known as The White Horse

Pathway downhill through woods at start of walk.

Kit's Coty House.

Stone, a long barrow marker stone. Carry on downhill to the flat, go over the bridge passing a car garage on the left heading for a petrol garage. Bear right with the path just before the garage, going up the slope and bear round walking on a gravel path as it climbs. Coming out to a road, turn left going downhill passing the Lower Bell Pub, then look out for steps approx. 300yards along the road on the left going into the woods. Go down the steps, through a Sycamore canopy to a junction where turn right, going uphill passing foxholes on the side of the mud path, before coming out onto the road. TAKE CARE IN CROSSING OVER. Cross over directly opposite heading uphill (path signed); a steep climb through Chestnut, Sycamore and Ash with dense cover.

As the path begins to flatten out bear left through an opening into the field where the Kit's Coty House stands in its majestic surroundings. Back out on the path, continue up to concrete steps. At the top turn left walking along the road to a footbridge crossing. Go up and over the road, then bear left with the path walking through a tiny section of nature's own garden, before coming out onto the road by a bus stop. Walk along 20 yards and bear right into the woods, on a gravel path, heading up a steep incline surrounded by dense tree cover and a wooden fence on the left. At the top turn left, walking along Warren Road and at the bend in the road bear round walking along Mill Lane passing the pub. Cross over the road, walk over the bridge and bear left into the car park.

A Sliver of the North Downs (Old and New)

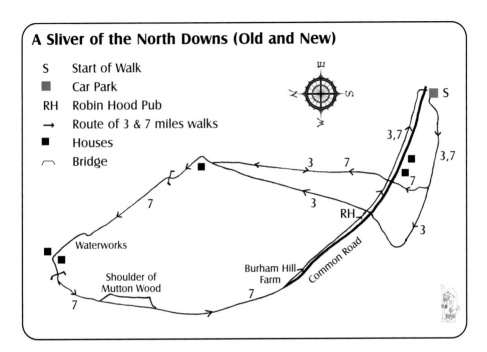

S   Start of Walk
■   Car Park
RH   Robin Hood Pub
→   Route of 3 & 7 miles walks
■   Houses
⌒   Bridge

Access/parking: as Ancient Stones

Map Reference: OS Explorer 148. GR743621

Distance:	7 miles. Short ➤ 3 miles
Time:	3½ hours. Short ➤ 1½ hours.
Terrain:	Field walking, mud paths, concrete paths, long gradual climb up.
Refreshments:	None on route.

Route Directions - Old and New

WALK 2 Start of Long/Short Walk. From the car park walk across to the bench and information board. Carry on walking on the grass path, (Burham Down), passing a bench and a gate on the right that leads out to the road. Stay on the path as it goes through trees and then slopes down passing more benches, with breathtaking views over the valley. Coming to a gate go through and turn left going downhill on a concrete path, walking through a dense canopy of Beech and Ash. At the junction (short➤ carry straight on) bear right heading uphill on a steep winding concrete path. Once at the top cross over the road and continue straight on, walking on a grass path through crop fields, heading for the woods in the far corner. Bear right heading into woods then turn left walking on a mud path heading into more dense Chestnut and Oak woods. At the junction go straight on, going down a step onto another mud path walking through

View by Shoulder of Mutton Wood.

dense woods. Stay on the path as it meanders then slowly descends through Yew trees, before coming out into the open, where newly planted trees are a feature. Coming onto a concrete path (short ➤ see path on left) bear right then left, passing a house on the left with the railway line to the right. Stay on the path as it climbs heading for the bridge ahead. Go over the bridge and bear left at the bollards heading down with the railway line on the left and wildlife banks on the right. Continue along the path going through stone bollards, then bear right going up onto the flat, then down the slope to a gate. Go through the gate passing the waterworks house on the left and continue on down to a group of houses. Bear left going up on a concrete path, passing between the houses with an oast house over on the right and continue up to a bridge crossing the railway line. Stay on the grass/mud path as it climbs bearing round onto a narrow grass path, with crop fields on the right and Shoulder of Mutton Wood on the left.

SHORT WALK Follow the directions from the car park to the junction through Burham Common. At the junction ➤ carry straight on to the next junction walking through a canopy of Beech, Ash and Holly. Turn right going uphill and at the top cross over the road heading downhill towards the Robin Hood pub. Continue on down the path walking through woods of Chestnut, Oak and Beech on a mud path, slowly descending before coming out onto a more open pathway with fencing each side. Reaching the bottom go over the stile and bear right heading uphill on the grass path before heading into the dark expanse of the Yew woods. Stay on the wide mud path at it climbs meandering through more Chestnut and Oak woods. Once on the flat, as the woods thin out, turn right heading out onto an open field. Staying on the mud path cross the field onto the road. Turn left walking along the road passing Burham Common on the right and some houses before reaching the entrance to the car park on the right.

Pathway down to railway line.

The White Horse Experience (Nr. Maidstone)

In the year 2000, twenty thousand trees of Oak, Ash, Silver Birch, Wild Cherry and Crab Apple were planted to help create the versatile surround of the White Horse Woods, which enhance the already stunning views from the top of Detling Hill over the North Downs and, given time, the whole area will look as it did hundreds of years ago, completely wooded.

Thurnham Castle stands over to the left of the woods in a majestic surrounding of ancient walls and earthworks, protected by the steep slope of the Downs. This castle is a ring-work and bailey castle (the ring-work is a raised roughly circular earthwork forming the strong point of the castle, bailey signifies a courtyard). A stone wall and towers were probably built on top of the earthwork, as remains of curtain walls can be seen along the north and west sides of the site. Bases of two square towers have been found, one at the northwest corner of the bailey, the other halfway along the west curtain. The bailey or outer court was protected by a gatehouse and a defensive wall where living quarters and other buildings were situated, allowing day-to-day tasks of cooking, washing, butchering and tending livestock, with the gatehouse being the main entrance into the castle complex. Stephen de Thurnham and his brother Robert held the castle in the twelfth century returning from the crusades with Richard the Lionheart to live out their lives in the castle. By the fourteenth century the castle had passed to the Northwood family and then Rupert Corbie.

Thurnham Castle ruin.

The White Horse Experience - Walks 1 and 1A

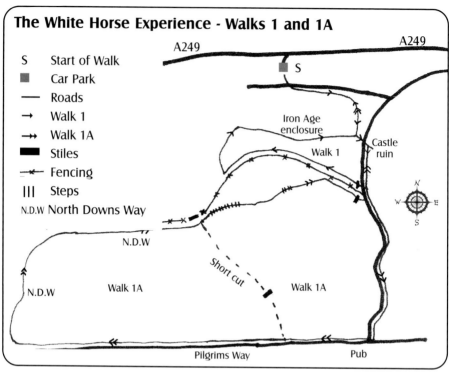

Legend:
- S — Start of Walk
- ■ — Car Park
- — — Roads
- → — Walk 1
- →→ — Walk 1A
- ■ — Stiles
- ×— — Fencing
- ||| — Steps
- N.D.W — North Downs Way

A249 · A249 · S · Iron Age enclosure · Walk 1 · Castle ruin · N.D.W · Short cut · N.D.W · Walk 1A · Walk 1A · Pilgrims Way · Pub

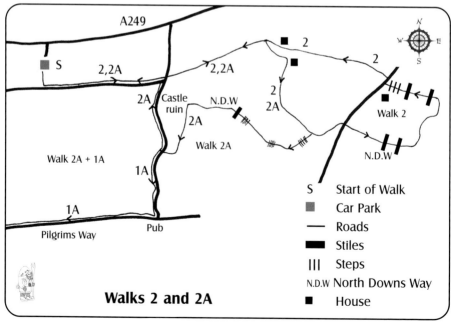

A249 · S · 2,2A · 2,2A · 2 · 2 · 2A · Castle ruin · N.D.W · 2 · 2A · 2A · Walk 2 · 2A · Walk 2A · N.D.W · Walk 2A + 1A · 1A · 1A · Pub · N.D.W · Pilgrims Way

Legend:
- S — Start of Walk
- ■ — Car Park
- — — Roads
- ■ — Stiles
- ||| — Steps
- N.D.W — North Downs Way
- ■ — House

Walks 2 and 2A

Access/parking: From the M2 turn off onto the A249 heading towards Maidstone; just past the garage turn left using the slip road. Car park charges 20p first hour. 50p all day. Sunday and Bank holiday £1 all day.

Map reference: OS Explorer 148. GR802587

Distance: Walk 1. 2$^1/_2$miles. Walk 1A. 7miles(short 5miles)
Walk 2. 6miles. Walk 2A. 5miles

Time: Walk 1. 60+ mins. Walk 1A 3$^1/_2$ hours (short 2$^1/_2$hours)
Walk 2. 3hours. Walk 2A. 2$^1/_2$hours.
WALK EXTRA, START WITH WALK 2A. COMING TO THE ROAD JUNCTION BELOW THURNHAM CASTLE, TURN LEFT GOING DOWNHILL, AND CONTINUE WITH WALK 1A (LONG).

Terrain: Road walking, concrete paths, grass paths, areas can be wet even in summer months. Stiles. Walk 1A. Very steep up, steep descent steps. Walk 2. Field walking, can be muddy all year, steep hills, many stiles. Walk 2A. Steps going down and up, field walking, grass paths, road walking.

Refreshments: Garage on main A249. Walk 1 and 1A Thurnham village en route, Black Horse Inn.

Route Directions

WALK 1 + 1A From the car park head towards the gate walking along a concrete path. Cross over the road, go through the gate and continue on the path going down to another gate. Go through and cross the road heading up the slope into the castle grounds. Then come out onto the road and turn left going downhill. **(Walk 1A stay on the road going downhill.)** After 200 yards turn right, then sharp right going over a stile. Follow the path beside the fence heading up. Further on, woods form an oval shape set into the valley. Reaching the edge of the woods go through a gate. Turn right, heading uphill on a grass path. Once at the top bear right heading for a concrete block going through a gate and onto a flat concrete path. A map is set in the concrete block. Continue on this path passing an area where many of the thousands of trees have been planted, before coming to a sign showing where an Iron Age enclosure once stood. Stay on the path as it continues round going downhill to the gate by the castle. Bear left with the path going uphill onto the flat, through a gate, cross the road and continue along the path with log edges back to the car park.

WALK 1A As Walk 1. Stay on the road going downhill passing a junction on the left, continue downhill (take care of traffic) to the road junction. Turn right passing the Black Horse Inn on the left and continue on, still descending, passing a group of houses before coming to open crop fields. (**SHORT CUT** turn into the field on the right walking

Iron Age enclosure.

through crops on a mud path heading uphill. Go over the stile and up a very steep incline to the top coming to wire fencing and a stile) **WALK 1A** continue along the road to a wide junction on the right (North Downs Way). Turn right walking up the grass/mud path and bear right walking beside the fence line slowly heading uphill with views of the Downs ahead. Stay on the path as it climbs up to an open stretch on the left after houses, where many fledgling trees can be seen, (this is part of the White Horse Woods plantation). Continue on along the flat to a stile. Still on the North Downs Way path, go past the stile, heading for the woods ahead and down the steps carved out of the mud/grass path beside the woods. Once at the bottom go over the stile and start to climb up again, heading for the clump of trees ahead, where there are steps again carved into the path to aid ascent. Stay on the path as it bears left cutting over the top of the scarp to the fence line on the flat. Coming onto a thin mud path, continue on to the end to a stile. Go over the stile out onto the road, and turn left to a gate with the castle ruin on the left, go through the gate on the right. Continue up the path to another gate. Go through, cross over the road and continue back along the path with log edges back to the car park.

WALK 2 From the car park, go along the concrete path to the gate and go through turning left onto the road, along to open fields opposite. Walk across the field on the mud path towards the transmitter pylon. Pass the pylon and a farm building on the left coming onto a road surface, turn right heading for a high haystack over to the left and woods ahead. Stay on the path to a junction and bear right passing woods on the left. Bear right at the gate and stay on the path to a gap in the tree line. Turn left heading into the woods on a mud path. As the path slowly descends through Ash, Beech, Chestnut coppice and brambles, bear left at the junction by the steps **(Walk 2A go down steps on the right)** passing metal gates each side of the path. Stay on the path

View across the Downs.

passing massive Rhododendron bushes on the left, going round a metal gate with an ivy clad wall on the left, down to a road. Cross over (on North Downs Way Path) and go straight up the steep path opposite. Climb up through woods onto the flat for 50 yards, before another steep climb up through Yew trees each side. Coming onto a thin mud path walk past fencing on the right which protects farmland crops, and woods on the left.

Continue on the path passing more Yew trees as the path descends steeply into the valley then coming to steps and a stile (high), go over and down the grass area to the next stile. Once over, turn left and follow the wide mud path, as it winds round and starts to climb with steps hewn out of the ground. At the top, beside a fallen tree turn left going uphill. Passing farm buildings on the right turn left onto the public footpath walking round a free-range pig farm enclosure (be aware electric fencing) on a mud grass path. As the path bears round left go over the stile on the right onto a grass path to the next stile. Go over the stile passing a farm on the left and a transmitter station over on the right. Continue on the path walking through woods passing more farm

Path at start of Walks 2 and 2a.

buildings on the left, before coming to steps leading onto a road. Turn right on road and 50 yards up turn left going into woods of Sycamore, Beech and Ash with fencing on the right and farm buildings at the back of the fields. Stay on the path passing a house, carry straight on ignoring junctions off to the left and right. As the path comes out into the open turn left then take the right fork onto the gravel path. Continue along the path passing the haystack and just before the farm building, bear left onto the mud path crossing the field to the opposite corner. Cross over and walk along the road to the gate back to the car park.

WALK 2A (On North Downs Way path) Turn right heading down the steps, walking under a canopy of Chestnut and Ash in sections of the path. Reaching the bottom, the 50yards of path on the flat is clear of trees, giving spectacular views across the Downs over to the left. Ahead the path climbs steeply going up steps. Stay on the grass/mud path as it goes up and down winding through dense woods. Continue on, down more steps, then up steps to a stile. Go over the stile onto a grass path walking beside the wire fencing at the bottom of the field, slowly climbing. Pass by an ancient tree by the fence line, follow the path round heading down into the valley to a gate. Go through and head downhill on a grass path walking beside the wire fence, heading into woodland. Walk past a group of trees on the left with dense vegetation on the right, and staying on the mud path continue round with the path to a gate on the right. (Go through gate and up steps to castle grounds).

Go straight on walking through a maze of trees and bracken with fencing on the right, to some steps. Go down the steps onto the road. (Take care). **EXTRA WALK** (Turn left and continue downhill to the junction, then right). Turn right going up the road passing the castle entrance on the right and onto the flat. Coming to the junction turn left walking along the concrete road to the park gate, go through and back along the path to the car park.

Cuxton's Secret Garden (Ranscombe Reserve)

This area of 560 acres is a jewel in the crown of the North Downs escarpment, nestling within rolling hills, allowing all to explore a classic landscape that has not greatly altered since the eighteenth century. Woodlands, arable fields and chalk grassland allow a rich diversity of wildlife to flourish in the midst of a working farm. The farm has been a recognised place to find wild plants for hundreds of years, with a number of rare plants like the Ground Pine, Hairy Mallow and the Meadow Clary which was first recorded in the area in 1699. Another national rarity found on the reserve in great quantities is the Broad-leaved Cudweed, along with species of orchid including Fly, Lady and Man.

A section of arable land on the far western side of the reserve is a natural haven for annual plants where the Narrow-fruited Corn-salad, Night-flowering Catchfly and the Blue Pimpernel can all be seen along with the very rare Corncockle plant. Woodland areas have their own distinct character with Bluebells and the Early Purple Orchid scattered over the woodland floor, while the chalk grassland areas allow the Wild Liquorice, Clustered Bellflower and the Horseshoe Vetch to flourish. Further over to the west the Mausoleum built in 1783 for the third Earl of Darnley was once a magnificent building of Portland stone with red marble facings and Doric columns. Although sadly neglected it still holds its own in the annals of important buildings in Kent, and is now being restored to its former glory.

View across the Downs.

Cuxton's Secret Garden (Near Strood)

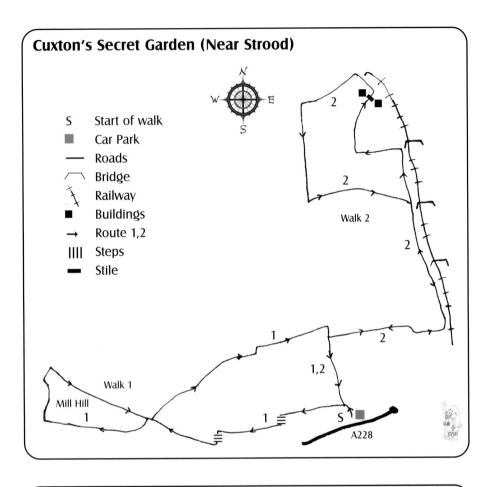

S   Start of walk
 ■ Car Park
— Roads
⌒ Bridge
Railway
■ Buildings
→ Route 1,2
|||| Steps
▬ Stile

Walk 2

Walk 1

Mill Hill

A228

Access/parking: From the M2 turn off onto the A228. At the first roundabout go straight over. At the next roundabout take the second turning heading for Cuxton. Go along 50 yards, turn right into the car park.

Map reference: OS Explorer 163. GR718674

Distance: Walk 1. 4 miles. Walk 2. 4 miles

Time: Walk 1. 2 hours. Walk 2. 2+ hours

Terrain: Grass slopes, grass/mud paths, steps, field walking. Mud paths can be slippery after rain and in winter.

Refreshments: Pub in Cuxton village 1/2 mile from car park.

Route Directions

WALK 1 From the car park walk up the concrete path going round and, looking back as the path climbs, seeing the Medway bridge and the River Medway. Halfway up an opening on the left leads into an open crop field with a set path round the top. Follow the path round to a gate in the opposite corner by the railway line, go through the gate, down the steps, turn right, go up 10 yards and up the steps on the left into a grazing field. Follow the grass path as it slowly climbs, walking beside the fence by the railway line. Continue straight on going downhill staying by the edge of the field to a gate on the left. Go through the gate, down the steps and turn right walking on a concrete path for 50 yards before coming to crop fields. Continue along the mud path walking between the fields with a chalk grass area over to the left. Go straight on at the junction then 500 yards further on turn left on a mud path heading for the woodland. Turn right in the woods walking up Mill Hill on a winding mud path between

Mausoleum.

Maple, Silver Birch and Beech. Continue climbing, taking the right fork at the V-junction in Bishops Wood, eventually coming to a bench on the top.

Continue on the flat, bearing to the right and climb up steps out onto open fields. Turn right walking round the edge of the field by the woods to a gate. Go through the gate, heading downhill through crop fields to the junction. Turn left on a wide mud path heading downhill, going through a tunnel of trees then, coming out between open crop fields, continue on the path to the junction near the telegraph poles. At the junction turn left, follow the path round heading uphill passing a bench where the views are once again stunning. Continue uphill to a turnstile gate, go through and stay on the mud path as it levels out then goes through an arch of trees. Bear left with the mud path passing the farm on the left, continue straight on to a concrete road. Turn right going along the road and then downhill passing the junction turned into at start of the walk, carry on back down to the car park.

Section of path on walk 1.

WALK 2 From the car park walk up the concrete path out onto the flat and carry on to the junction just before the farmhouse. Turn right walking over crop fields on a thin mud path heading downhill towards the railway line and woods. Go through the woods coming out into a grass area with a railway

Route on walk 1 to woodland area.

bridge ahead, turn left by the post just before the bridge, onto a grass path heading uphill. Continue going up on a mud path walking beside the main railway line on the right and woods on the left, passing a bridge on the right. Carry on up to a section on the flat where wooden posts line the path in front of the second bridge. Ignore the turning off to the left, continue straight on up going through wooden posts on a wide grass path, still beside the railway line passing Chestnut coppice woods. Reaching the log fence and posts go through, shortly after turn left onto a wide mud path, with fencing both sides going uphill away from the railway line. Continue going up passing Buddleia bushes, Beech and Horse Chestnut trees as the path winds aiding the ascent. At the junction on the flat turn right going downhill passing a pond over to the left and heading towards a house; go over the stile then turn left, staying on the gravel path walking between houses, and straight on heading towards a bridge. Turn left by the bridge walking along the mud path between the railway line and wooden fenced paddocks where horses are kept from the nearby stables. Stay on the mud path as it bears left away from the railway line still walking round the paddocks on the left and woodland to the right. Coming to the far corner go right, through the gate heading into the woods, go on 50 yards to another gate then left going uphill. Ignoring paths leading off, climb up through woods of Silver Birch, Chestnut and Beech. The last steep 20 yards

Pathway up from car park, walks 1 and 2.

brings you out onto the flat with bracken and gorse bushes each side of the stony path. At the junction turn left walking along a wide grass path, continue straight on at the next junction heading into thicker woodland. Continue going down on the winding mud path passing coppiced Chestnut before coming out by the bridge where the wooden posts line the path. Turn right and continue going downhill on the path walked up earlier passing the bridge and down to the grass area. Go downhill crossing the grass area to a stony path where turn right heading for the woods. Once through the woods the mud path climbs up through crop fields onto a concrete path. Turn left walking on the flat heading for a tree line and stay on the path as it descends and winds down the hill to the car park.

Pathway up from car park on walk 2.

Darland Banks Scramble (Gillingham)

Darland is an area of superb chalk and grassland scrub on a steep ridge on the North Downs covering an area of 35 acres. Designated a Site of Special Scientific Interest in 1968 because of its rich and diverse flora and fauna, the area lost its national status because of the invasive Hawthorn scrub and was granted a Nature Reserve status in 1989. Part of the walk includes the Ambley Wood, an area not included in the reserve status but equally respected for its flora and fauna. Hornbeam, Sweet Chestnut, Ash, Field Maple along with Wild Privet, Dog Rose, Blackthorn and Wayfaring tree are all seen on the edge of the wood. Greater Spotted Woodpeckers, Green Woodpeckers as well as Blackcaps, Robins, Chiffchaffs and the Song Thrush have all been seen in the wood together with many species of butterfly.

An important discovery in the area is of the dormouse, now very rare in Britain. The downland is, because of its chalk grassland, well known for its orchids including the green Man Orchid and the pinkish Pyramidal Orchid, as well as many herbs like Marjoram, Wild Basil, Wild Thyme, Salad Burnet, and Hairy Violet all mixing in with the bright orange/yellow of Bird's-foot Trefoil and Kidney Vetch, along with the white Oxeye Daisy and pink Knapweed. These flowers attract many species of butterfly like the Brown Argus, Chalkhill Blue and the Marbled White, as well as bees, hoverflies and grasshoppers. In June and July glow-worms can be seen on a night-time walk while the rare Roesel's bush-cricket can be found in the longer vegetation. All along the walk the views into the valley and across the downland are exceptional in their diverse colours and natural elements.

Path across top of Reserve on short walk.

Darland Banks Scramble (Gillingham)

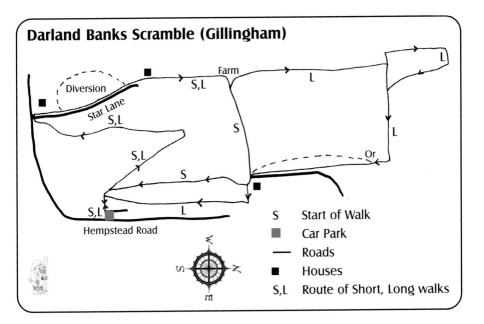

S — Start of Walk
■ (grey) — Car Park
— — Roads
■ (black) — Houses
S,L — Route of Short, Long walks

Access/parking: From the M2 take the A278 towards Gillingham. Turn left at the second roundabout and left again at the mini-roundabout. Go along 50 yards and turn right into Hoath Close. Free parking.

Map Reference: OS Explorer 163. GR796655

Distance: Short walk 2 miles. Diversion +1 mile. Long walk 4 miles.

Time: Short walk 1+ hours. Diversion +$\frac{1}{2}$ hour. Long walk 2hours.

Terrain: Steep slopes down. Steep paths up. Grass paths. Road walking. Mud paths slippery in wet weather. Stiles.

Refreshments: Gillingham town 1 mile from car park.

Route Directions

From the car park walk down the slope to a concrete path, bearing right to a gate. Go through heading downhill on a grass path until reaching a stile. Once over the stile bear left walking on a mud path with tree cover each side often creating a canopy overhead. The path slowly climbs then bears right heading downhill and through a small patch of trees coming out onto a green beside the road. Bear right staying on the grass path walking downhill towards the house on the corner. Turn right into Star Lane beside the house and continue along the road (take care of traffic). **(Diversion)** At the bend in the

Steep chalk path on long walk.

road turn left going through a gate and walk over the field bearing left as the path climbs. The path heads into the lower part of Grove Wood, where at the junction turn right to come out onto the open fields and down to the main path. **(diversion end)** Where the road ends in front of the farmhouse bear left onto a grass path walking beside the farmhouse. Continue straight on, walking between crop fields on a thin mud/grass path to the back of Darland Farm.

SHORT WALK At the junction by the wall turn right and start to climb up the steep slope on a concrete/mud path. At the top climb over the stile and go straight over the road

View from the road into Reserve, long walk.

heading uphill on a concrete path passing a house on the left. At the top of the hill bear right going over a stile and onto the top of the Downs. (This path can be slippery in wet weather). Stay on the mud path as it winds along the top of the reserve going over another stile and dipping down slightly, passing through Rose Hip bushes before climbing back up. Stay on the path as it slowly climbs up onto the flat. Coming to a gate go through and bear left going uphill on the concrete path back to the car park.

LONG WALK At the junction by the wall go through the gate on the right heading uphill. Look out for a wide mud path on the left about 200 yards up. Turn left onto the path going through dense canopy Pines out onto a mud path with fencing and a gate on the right. (Take care of the fencing as part is electrified). Stay on the path as it winds towards a gate. Go through the gate and turn left, down 20 yards and then right heading uphill on a mud path. At the junction turn right walking over the Downs to a stile. Climb over the stile and turn left uphill on a chalk path. Go through the next gate and continue up now on a very steep chalk path climb. Once at the top turn right walking along the very top on a mud path. OR turn right going through the gate 50 yards on, walking on a thin mud path going through gates and winding round clumps of trees, with stunning views into the valley below. BOTH PATHS LEAD UP TO THE GATE. Go through the gate onto a concrete path and continue uphill passing a house on the left. At the top ignore the stile on the right and continue up to a gate. Go through the gate and turn right, walking on a mud path into a green haven from where stunning views can be seen. Continue along the path passing tiny inlets on the left where new growth is flourishing, and onto a concrete path. Turn left going up into the road where the car is parked.

Path uphill from farm of short walk.

Northward Hill Uncovered (Hoo Peninsula)

Northward Hill combines a national Nature Reserve with woodland and marshes to make the most scenic, largest and oldest reserve in Kent. The area also supports the UK's largest heronry with more than 150 pairs of Grey Herons visiting each year. This is in a spectacular area of woodland where the birds nest from March to June each year. From the hill covered by ancient Oaks, down through scrubland to the open marsh areas, a vast diversity of natural flora and fauna along with wildlife accompany every step, as well as remains of Roman pottery.

The different seasons bring their own colour and diversity of nature from the emerging greens in spring, with a greater depth to them in summer mixed in with the pink of the Rosebay Willowherb. Butterflies, reptiles and insects are evident amongst the trees, plants and grasses at this time as are a variety of birds through the autumn and into winter when Hen Harriers, Peregrine, Buzzard, Merlin, Ducks and Bewick's swans can be seen.

The long walk shows up numerous varieties of plants and flowers in and around the stream such as the yellow Common Ragwort, pink Centaury, Oxeye Daisy and Golden Rod - ideal for many different butterflies. The whole area contains some breathtaking scenery.

River on long walk, near heronry.

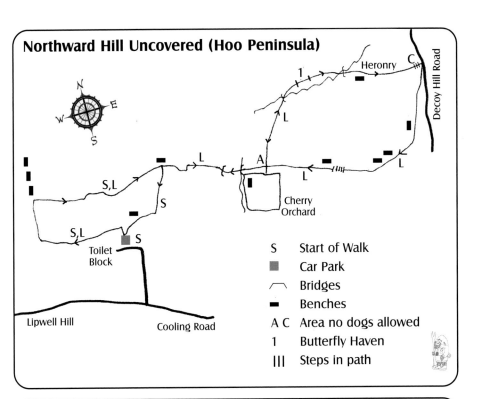

Northward Hill Uncovered (Hoo Peninsula)

Key:

S	Start of Walk
■	Car Park
⌒	Bridges
▬	Benches
A C	Area no dogs allowed
1	Butterfly Haven
|||	Steps in path

Access/parking: From the A228 turn up Christmas Lane (2nd roundabout) heading for High Halstow. Bear left in the village, go along Cooling Road, staying on the road as it winds. Going over a hill, look out for a bungalow on the right. Turn up this road but continue on following the track as it bears left round to a barn area. Free parking.

Map reference: OS Explorer 163. GR767764

Distance: Short walk: 1¼ miles. Long walk: 6 miles.

Time: Short walk: 40 minutes minimum. Long walk: 3 hours +

Terrain: Short walk: grass paths, gradual climbing, uneven paths. Long walk: grass paths, stiles, steep climb, mud paths. Extra walk through Cherry orchard.

Refreshments: Toilets in barns in car park. Pub and shop in High Halstow 1 mile away.

**Please note: dogs are not allowed on the short or long walk.
The long walk incorporates the heronry.**

Route Directions

SHORT WALK From the car park go past the information boards onto a concrete path walking past tall grasses and thistles. Turn left with the path and continue on heading uphill on a wide grass/stone path with trees on the left, grasses intertwined with Rosebay Willowherb giving a spectacle that will continue with the walk. Once at the top, leaning over the fence to the left is the area where Roman pottery was found. Continue on along the top of the ridge passing a path on the right, coming to 3 benches on the left from where there are spectacular views across the marshes. Go back to the path passed earlier and continue downhill on the grass/clover/heather path again passing through a miniature wilderness. Turn right and continue on the more uneven path as it winds round to the left passing Silver Birch and Chestnut trees onto a gravel path. Go straight over back onto a grass path slowly climbing, walking through scattered Blackberry and Gorse bushes to the top. Bear left behind the bench going downhill through a corridor of gorse on a grass path. On reaching the flat bear right with the path then left coming to the concrete path at the start of the walk. Turn left and walk back to the car park.

LONG WALK Follow the directions of the short walk climbing up the hill through scattered Blackberry and Gorse bushes to the top. Walking behind the bench continue straight on the grass path going downhill, staying on the path as it winds round onto a mud path and out to a gravel path. Cross over and bear right walking on the grass path, passing fencing on the left, towards a bridge, where the water has been dammed each side to create water holes for insects and birds. Stay on the path crossing over the bridge coming to another small bridge. Cross over onto a wide grass track, walk up about 100 yards before seeing a stile on the left and a Cherry orchard on the right.

Ruin on valley floor.

Cherry orchard.

Walk through Cherry orchard, go through the entrance gate designed like traditional orchard ladders, over a metal grille heading straight on with massive aged Cherry trees on the right and fencing on the left. Stay on the grass path as it bears right going between the two sections of orchard and continues round with a stream on the left. Coming up to the next bend look out for an intricately carved bench made from a single oak tree on the left. Further up on the left and right are remnants of artwork created from twigs found on the floor of the woods. Follow the path round back to the gate, then cross over the grass path to the stile. Go over the stile into a field going straight across and then bearing right to a bridge. Cross over the bridge and stay on the path walking beside the stream, round the edge of the field. Bear right with the stream heading for a stile in the corner. Go over the stile on a mud path into a butterfly haven, with the stream still on the right and continue through to another stile. Go over the stile, bear right, go along 50 yards to the next stile, go over and continue along the path walking beside the river to the following stile. Go over and cross the bridge straight ahead bearing round on the mud path into a wooded area. Come out into the open onto a grass path as it climbs.

After a short distance there is a fantastic view over to the heronry on the left. Continue on up the hill ignoring paths off to the left. At the top go up the steps to the stile and, climbing over, go straight ahead over another stile, heading into dense woodland. Stay on the thin mud path as it climbs up to an opening before heading back into a dense pine canopy with roots creating steps in the path. Reaching the top climb over the stile coming out onto a crop field where bear right walking round the edge of the field and then bear right coming to another field. Continue along the track to a gap and turn right following the path as it heads towards woods opposite. Go through the gate, with woodland on the left and open grassland over to the right, with views of the Thames in the background and continue to climb up on the grass path to a welcome bench on the top of Northward Hill. From the bench, carry on round the top to a gap in the trees on the right. Turn right and go through the gate 20 yards in, now walking in deep mature woodland. Turn left onto a concrete/mud path going downhill, then climbing back up, passing majestic Oaks each side before coming to two benches where the scenery is totally captivating. Staying on the path as it winds round to a junction, head downhill as the path changes to gravel with log borders, then steps, before opening up to magnificent views across the marshes and beyond. Continue on down the wide grass path until reaching the flat, passing the stile crossed earlier. Stay on the path walking back on the grass over the bridge, then bear round over to another bridge which cross over. Continue on, passing the fencing to the concrete road; cross over and bear left back onto a grass path, as it winds round, then starts to climb. At the top walk behind the bench, bear left heading downhill on a grass path passing gorse bushes. Once on the flat bear right then left onto the concrete path at the start of the walk. Turn left into the car park.

Start of short walk going uphill.

Cliffe Marshes Phenomenon (Hoo Peninsula)

Cliffe pools and marshes are the result of many years of struggle to protect this section of the Thames Estuary as the area was used as a dump. It now has the highest level of international wildlife protection and is a magnificent example of fauna and flora taking over and flourishing. The large saline lagoons that account for more than 3% of the total in the U.K. are full of microscopic life, which attract wild ducks in winter. Wading birds like the Avocet, Redshank and Lapwing nest and rear their young in the spring, while tiny islands created within the lagoons allow birds to rest and feed, as well as areas of salt-marsh. Scrubland where Buddleia, Blackberry and Wild Rose along with Yarrow, Wild Carrot, Bird's-foot Trefoil, Ribbed Melilot, Chicory, red and white clover all flourish, encourage bumblebees, many species of butterfly like the Small White, Meadow Brown, Common Blue, Tortoiseshells, Peacocks and the Red Admiral. Small mammals like the fox, squirrel, dormouse and rabbit all play their part in the evolving reserve.

Cliffe Fort straddles along the River Thames estuary, built in 1860 and still a dominating feature on the walk with its torpedo channels still visible. At low tide the wreck of both a ship and pier are highly visible and show the workings of the land gone by. Another feature of the walk is the eerie vision of tankers passing by as the sea wall obscures all but the funnels.

Stopping area on short walk.

Cliffe Marshes Phenomenon (Hoo Peninsula)

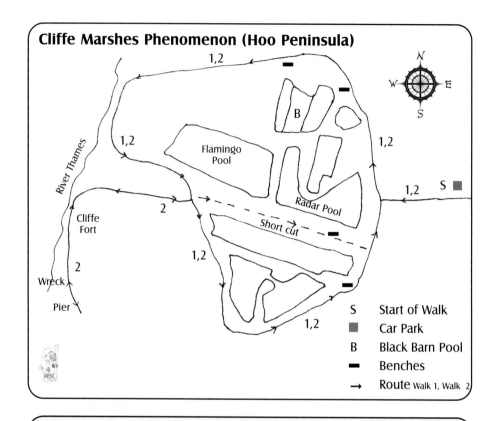

S   Start of Walk
■   Car Park
B   Black Barn Pool
—   Benches
→   Route Walk 1, Walk 2

Access/parking: Head for Cliffe village on the B2000. Go through village passing a church on the left. Follow road round and down a concrete road. Park on the grass. Other parking opposite church.

Map Reference: OS Explorer 163. GR735768

Distance: Walk 1. 4 miles. Walk 2.Cliffe fort+ 6 miles

Time: Walk 1. 2 hours+. Walk 2.Cliffe fort 3hours+

Terrain: Walk 1. flat concrete paths, mud paths, 1 stile.
Walk 2. as main walk plus uneven paths, grass paths.

Refreshments: Available at The Six Bells pub by church. Shop and toilets also in the village.

Note: Short cut path cuts off approx 1½ miles. The flat path winds between two iridescent pools seen through gaps in the wild rose bushes. Further along the path an opening on the left, fenced, gives protection against falling in the water, as it allows you to reach the 'beach' and watch both the tide and birds on the water and the tiny islands.

Route Directions

WALK 1 After parking the car by the green, continue straight on following the road going through concrete bollards. Stay on the wide uneven concrete path passing fields on the right where cattle are grazed to help maintain the area, with a stream running beside the path. On the left Ash, Beech and Hawthorn trees along with bracken and Wild Rose bushes help create a mini-oasis for birds and other insects. Coming to the junction turn right onto the concrete path walking beside the Radar Pool. Continue along the path passing a barn on the right, then bear left to a tarmac path leading up a short hill, to a viewing point looking over Black Barn Pool. Stay on the path passing another tarmac ramp going up to Pipe Pool mound, and continue on, to an iron gate. Climb over the stile beside the gate and carry on, walking on an uneven gravel path passing an area of salt-marsh on the left. Coming up to a junction turn left with the sea wall on the right. Stay on the path passing steps in the sea wall leading to the River Thames and bear left walking between high mounds before spotting the 'beach' of Flamingo Pool on the left. Continue round seeing much more of Flamingo Pool with a low wall on the right at the top of a grass ramp.

Coming to a wide section of path, **(diversions »to the left a path goes through scrubland providing a short cut. Walk 2 on the right goes up the grass ramp to the wall.)** continue straight on as the path changes to mud/sand, winding between pools of iridescent blue on the left and grassland to the right. As houses come into view over to the far right go through a fence onto a concrete road and turn directly left going round a black gate onto a concrete path. Carry on, with the pools on the left and woods of Ash and Beech on the right. Stay on the path as it winds round to another black gate; go through a swing gate to the side and continue on, passing a concrete path going up to The Pinnacle, a viewpoint that opens up a vast expanse of water that's worth the stop. Walk on passing a path on the left **(end of short cut)** before coming to another black gate. Walk round the side of the gate and go on for another 50 yards before turning right going back down the wide uneven gravel path past the stream to the car park.

Cliffe Fort.

WALK 2 Go up the ramp to the wall. Climb over the wall and bear left walking along the sand path in between gorse and grass to a path on the right. Go along this mud path between mudflats on

Wreck of ship at low tide. Walk 2.

each side. Coming onto a thin concrete path, pass a wall on the right into a yard. Continue straight on passing open water on the right then bear round with the path heading towards the dock. Go down the steps into the yard and turn left going down a wide sand path, turning right after 50 yards into the Cliffe Fort area. (The actual fort is unsafe to enter) Go through the gate walking up past the fort, onto a grass path by the contour of the river. Turn left, walking along the path to a wreck and relics of wood which were once the jetty, then follow the path (section of Saxon Shore Way), round the

Beach of flamingo pool.

contours of Higham Creek and Higham Saltings, before returning by the same path back to the fort. Stay on the path coming to steps going down then back up. These steps are at the rear of the torpedo ramp used in the Second World War as protection from invading vessels coming up the Thames.

Pass by ruins of sections of the fort as the path comes back into the yard entered earlier. Cross over the yard and back up the steps onto the mud path going round past the wall and open water onto the thin grass path. Pass the mudflats, leading back to the sand path and bear left walking through the gorse bushes onto the ramp. Climb over the wall, go down the grass ramp to the path, and turn right following the directions of walk 1 back to the car park.

Looking over the lake to short-cut path.

Cooling's Classic Encounter (Hoo Peninsula)

The tiny village of Cooling is dominated by its 14th century castle, built to protect the village from French invaders, and the church of St James. John de Cobham instructed builders to fortify the manor into a castle to protect the village from a second attack by the French, after the first sortie had shown how defenceless the area was and that the route into London was wide open. Today the castle is on private land and not a visitor attraction, but the outside and some of the original building work is still evident from the road entrance. St James church has a special significance in the way of its graveyard. By the church entrance thirteen tiny graves, lying in two groups beside each other, are the result of 'The Ague' or 'Marsh Fever' (a mosquito-borne disease), where a complete family were wiped out in the 1770s.

This area is also Charles Dickens' country and his book 'Great Expectations' evokes the atmosphere from seeing the tiny graves and absorbing the melancholic aura on the marshes and surrounding areas. The area also has orchards of Pear and Cherry trees, which have been cultivated since the sixteenth century with the annual harvest being collected by village people. It was not until the early twentieth century that 'picking' became a popular holiday for people from the East End, making a little money to buy that extra something, with whole families camping in the nearby fields.

St. James Church and graves.

Cooling's Classic Encounter (Hoo Peninsula)

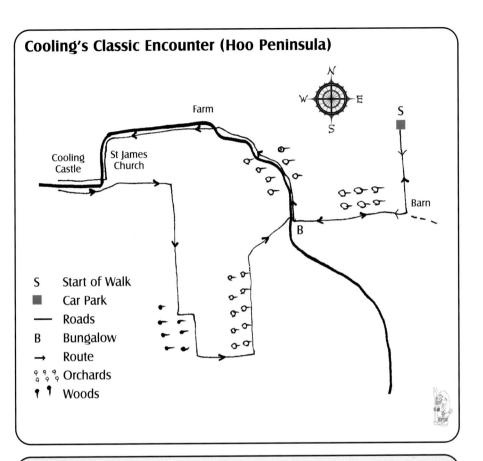

S   Start of Walk
■   Car Park
—   Roads
B   Bungalow
→   Route
♀♀♀   Orchards
🌲🌲   Woods

Access/parking: From the A228 turn up Christmas Lane (2nd roundabout) heading for High Halstow. Bear left in the village, go along Cooling Road staying on the road as it winds. Going over a hill, look out for a bungalow on the right. Turn up this road but continue on following the track as it bears left round to farm buildings. Free parking.

Map Reference: OS Explorer 163. GR767764.

Distance: 3 miles. Extra walk, short, 1 mile. Extra walk, long, 5 miles.

Time: 1½ hours. Extra walk, short, 30 minutes. Extra walk, long, 2½- 3 hours.

Terrain: Road walking. (Care needed in parts) grass paths, mud paths, hill climb. Extra walks, see Northward Hill Uncovered P44.

Refreshments: Toilets in the barn in the car park. Pub Horseshoe & Castle open all day for food in Cooling village.

Route Directions

From the car park walk back up the road past Pear orchards and turn right onto the road. (Take care, winding road and possible fast cars). Passing more orchards on the right continue round the bends to a path just before the farm. Continue on past the farm, cross over passing the Horseshoe & Castle pub on the left. Stay on the path walking past the few houses in the village, then pass the village hall and continue on round a bend with St James church on the left. After visiting the church and graveyard come out by the main gate and cross the road going straight ahead along the road for 200 yards to Cooling castle. From the castle, walk back to the church, heading for the gate where bear right going down the path beside the churchyard wall with a crop field on the right. Continue round the edge of the crop field to a main junction. Turn right onto a grass path going slowly uphill heading for woods. Bear left onto a well-trodden mud path heading up and round as it climbs up the hill. (Can be slippery in wet weather). At the top bear right and 10 yards on, bear left walking round the edge of a field with excellent views of the marshes. Follow the grass path round the edge of the field with the Stoney Rocks Pear orchard on the left and staying on this path, climb up the hill to the top. Bear left walking beside a line of Poplar trees which were planted to protect the Pear orchard from the wind,(the wind can cause the fruit to rub against twigs and cause unsightly blemishes). Continue along the path as it starts to descend. At the corner bear left on a grass path, seeing telegraph poles ahead, to the next junction where bear left going downhill towards the road with the bungalow ahead. Once there cross over and go up the road past the orchard at the beginning of the walk and turn left with the path at the barn following it round for another 300 yards to the car park.

Road and orchard on start and return of walk.

Cooling Castle.

Path uphill heading for woodland.

St Mary's Magnitude (Hoo Peninsula)

St Mary Hoo is a tiny village with one pub, scattered houses, a church (which is now a private house), farms and open marshland. Walking on mainly flat paths round the headland of north Kent the wildlife and landscapes are noteworthy. The area was once a favoured spot for smugglers with small bays allowing illegal goods to be landed and transported inland.

A famous poem by Rudyard Kipling conjures up the atmosphere of the area: 'If you wake at midnight, and hear a horse's feet, don't go drawing back the blind, or looking in the street, them that asks no questions isn't told a lie, watch the wall, my darling, while the gentlemen go by! Five and twenty ponies, trotting through the dark, brandy for the parson, 'baccy for the clerk; laces for a lady, letters for a spy, watch the wall, my darling, while the gentlemen go by!' Sheep were kept on the marshes to cover the tracks of the horse and cart and an isolated building is still visible near Egypt Bay where goods were stored.

Many years after the smuggling gangs a different kind of ship was seen offshore around the bays. Stripped of its rigging, its decked patrolled by armed officers, the 'prison ship' was a sight seen by many and was the inspiration for Charles Dickens' 'Great Expectations' with the escaped prisoners on the marshes. Unlike the book many prisoners died from the filth and overcrowding, while some starved after losing rations to pay debts. Others rose above the degradation and carved model sailing ships in their own time; these are exhibited in the Rochester Guildhall Museum. The mudflats in St Mary's Bay and Egypt Bay are both excellent areas for birds with the salt-marsh providing safe roosting places. Dunlin and Curlews congregate in the winter with Redshank and Lapwings being seen in the summer months. Many of the plants seen on the flat coastal wall, and on the fields, like Viper's Bugloss, Heather, red and green Clover, Oxeye Daisy along with Sea Kale and Sea Astor - which was once used as an antidote for poisons in Elizabethan times - attract a variety of butterflies including the Large White and Red Admiral.

Please be aware that cows and calves can be in the lower fields in the summer months.

Beach area on short walk now covered by stones to prevent flooding.

St Mary's Magnitude (Hoo Peninsula)

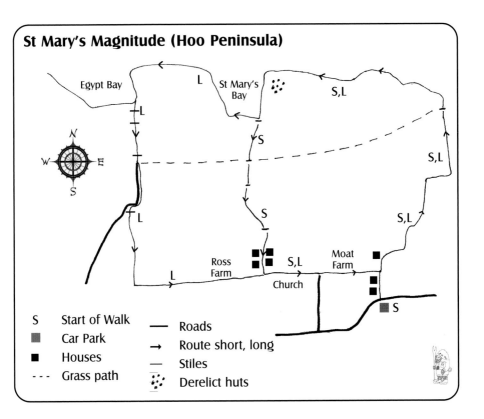

S Start of Walk	— Roads
■ Car Park	→ Route short, long
■ Houses	— Stiles
- - - Grass path	:·: Derelict huts

Access/parking: From the A289 from Rochester turn right onto the A228 towards Grain. Stay on this road into St Mary Hoo. Turn left on the bend into Fenn Street. Pass the pub on the right, carry on along the road going round a bend. On the left is a parking area in front of houses.

Map Reference: OS Explorer 163. GR812768

Distance: Short walk 7 miles. Long walk 11 miles.

Time: Short walk 3hours+. Long walk 5 hours+

Terrain: Short walk: grass paths, stone/mud paths, walking along sea wall. Steep climb up on return. Paths with rabbit holes. Long walk: As short walk, road walking. Many stiles.

Refreshments: No facilities on site. Pub in village open for meals.

Please note: in all seasons there can be a chilly wind on the sea wall.

Route Directions

SHORT WALK From the car park walk back to the corner and down the road passing houses on the left, and a crop field, before coming to a white gate. Go past the gate staying on the road as it winds round the edge of an enclosed field heading for houses. Pass by, walking to the end of the path and turn right at the junction. Go round the metal gate ahead onto a stone/mud path passing Sycamore, Ash and Hawthorn trees staying on the path as it bears left, and starts to descend. Carry straight on at the junction going down on a grass path walking between crop fields with views over the River Thames to Canvey Island, a spectacular sight. Coming to a junction with a dyke on the left and fencing ahead, turn right onto a wide grass path thick with clover. Pass a gate on the left with fencing on the right, and continue straight on bearing round with the path coming to reeds on the left with a view down the channel. Climb up the slope onto the top and turn left, walking along the top wall, on a stone/mud path. Down on the left the dyke follows the contour of the wall, allowing plants like Red Heather, Viper's Bugloss, Oxeye Daisy and Sea Kale to flourish. Continue along the path going over a stile passing a stony beach 200 yards long on the right. Go over another stile passing a groyne on the right. Another stony beach can be seen ahead on the right as the path winds and another stile needs climbing over. Passing another groyne over to the right, derelict huts are visible on the marsh on the left. Continue on the path passing West Point bearing left into St Mary's Bay. Over to the right the mudflats and salt-marsh attract many species of bird. Stay on the path going downhill to a junction, **(LONG WALK BEAR RIGHT)** go straight on, going over the stile onto a wide grass path, with a dyke and reeds on the left. Stay on the path to the junction, go over the stile opposite, walking straight ahead through a field to the opposite side and over the stile. Continue straight on walking on the grass path, climbing uphill on a steep incline

Huts are remains of army ammunition dump from 1900.

St. Mary's Parochial School (1868) on route to church in village.

heading for a clump of trees and a fence line. Go through the gate and bear left onto a stone/mud path still climbing up. Once at the top farm buildings are ahead with the top of the church visible behind the tree line. Bear right at the top going through a metal gate onto a concrete path, passing hay barns on the right and fields on the left. Continue straight on heading towards the church and bear round with the path, passing houses on the left with the church on the right. Pass a pink building, now a private house, with a plaque showing it was St Mary's Parochial School, built in 1868. ➳ Coming to a junction go straight on heading towards Moat Farm on a concrete road with Hall Road on the right. Bear right past the farmhouse going over a grass area and a stone/mud yard heading for a clump of trees opposite. Look for the opening in the tree line and head down the mud path walking through the dense canopy of trees. (Watch out on the path for rabbit borrows and small holes in the middle of the path, maybe covered by grass). Stay on the path as it winds and thins. Coming to a tiny slope, go up and round now walking between crop fields, with Hawthorn bushes as hedging, on a mud path with often high weeds and nettles each side. Continue on beside a fenced field with houses over to the left. Bear right walking round the fence to the road and the white gate at the start of the walk. Turn right walking down the road passing the crop field and then houses to where the car is parked.

LONG WALK (AT THE JUNCTION BEAR RIGHT) Stay on the grass path walking round the bay with the marshland on the right coming back up onto the sea wall. Continue with the contour of the wall. The path passes three more groynes before bearing left into Egypt Bay, where many a smuggling run was made. Stay on the path bearing left heading inland walking on top of the bank with a ditch on the left to a stile. Climb over and, bearing left, stay on a diagonal path heading for a double stile. Climb over both stiles and continue onto a stone/mud track then turn right.

Over to the left on the marshes an isolated building 'The Shades' was built especially to help with the landing of smuggled goods, which were transported from the boats to the house along brick tunnels from the shore, as tales go. Stay on the track to the road, go over the stile and follow the road round as it bears right then left. Coming to a footpath straight ahead on the bend go over the stile and climb up the steep hill to the crossroads at the top where turn left. Stay on the stone/mud path heading for the brown farmhouse of Newlands Farm, where in the summer months the large blue and green Emperor Dragonfly and the Black-tailed Skimmer can be seen. On reaching the farm go round the duck pond (not into the farmyard) and down a small flight of steps onto the road. As the road bends round to the left continue straight ahead on a stone/mud track heading towards the church in the distance. At the junction by the church go straight on ➤➤ (from this point) following the directions on the short walk back to the car park.

View from top path back across reedbeds.

Queendown Warren Saunter (Nr. Gillingham)

This area of chalk grassland is a Site of Special Scientific Interest, where low-growing wild flowers flourish in the poorer nutrient soil, often found on the steeper slopes of the Downs. The Warren is renowned for its variety of orchids found on the reserve from late spring when the rare Early Spider can be seen, followed by the Man, Fly, Fragrant, Pyramidal and Bee. By summer the area is awash with colour from the Cowslip, Yellowwort, reddish Sainfoin, Stemless Thistle and purple Wild Thyme. Several plants seen on the Warren have close associations with butterflies like the Common Blue; the rare Chalk Blue feed on the Horseshoe Vetch which is mainly found on chalk grassland. Rock Rose is the food plant for the Brown Argus caterpillar with Red Fescue grasses being eaten by Marbled White caterpillars. Autumn brings out blackberries and rosehips coupled with wild thyme, chestnuts and cobnuts in the woods.

The reserve also includes Potters Wood, an ancient woodland of Oak, Ash, Wild Cherry and Beech with Sweet Chestnut, Hazel and Hornbeam.

Pathway at start of walk, going through tree line.

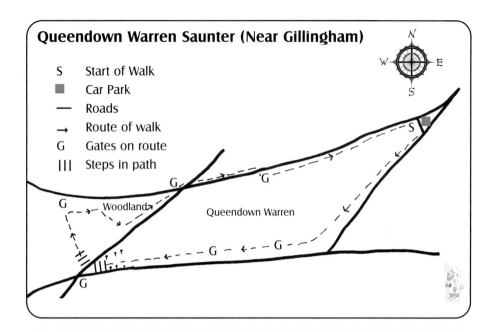

Queendown Warren Saunter (Near Gillingham)

S   Start of Walk
■   Car Park
—   Roads
→   Route of walk
G   Gates on route
||| Steps in path

Woodland

Queendown Warren

Access/Parking: From the M2 turn off at Junction 4 towards Gillingham. At the 1st roundabout turn right to Wigmore. Turn right again and carry on to roundabout signed Bredhurst. Turn right going under a bridge and over the M2. Turn next left into Kemsley Street Road, carry on for 1¹/₂ miles. Turn right for Hartlip. Parking approx. 1 mile along the road on the right.

Map Reference: OS Explorer 163. GR834633

Distance: 3 miles

Time: 1¹/₂ hours

Terrain: Grass paths, mud paths, road walking.

Refreshments: No facilities on site. Gillingham 3 miles. Hartlip 1 mile.

Route Directions

From the car park cross the road and go through the gate opposite, stay on the mud path, going through a canopy top then bear left on a grass path heading downhill, coming out into an open green paradise where views across the valley opposite of iridescent greens, mixed with yellow, white and pink/purple of flower tops are spectacular. Stay on the path going through the gate ahead and continue straight on. Then bear right going uphill on a mud/grass path, passing woods on the left and open grass areas. Continue on the grass path to a junction, take the left fork heading into woods on a thin mud path. Go through a gate and down the steps to the road. Cross over and almost directly opposite go up the step and start climbing, heading into deep canopy woods and thick undergrowth. The path comes out onto open grass, still on a gradual climb, and continues up past a vast Cobnut tree, its roots acting as steps on the mud path.

Path from stile into Warren, return path.

Continue on the path and just past the next ancient tree turn right, going uphill on a grass path which leads out onto an open grass area on top of the valley. Walk towards the back of the field going round the top following the contour of a wire fence. Go through the gate and continue on the path going downhill, passing a great variety of wild flowers, including rare orchids. Follow the path round climbing back uphill and head for the right-hand corner. Go through the gate and turn right onto the road. Go straight on along the road passing a parking

View from top of hill across the Downs.

area on the left to an entrance gate on the right; go through and turn left walking along the top of the valley as the path weaves through brambles and patches of wild flowers back to the mud path. Continue straight on going under the canopy of trees to the gate opposite where the car is parked.

Old and Bold Explored (Lullingstone, Eynsford)

Lullingstone Park is situated just outside the picture-postcard village of Eynsford nestling in the Darent Valley. Many tiny villages like Eynsford may have a 'Sparepenny Lane' as a country lane. The origin of the name dates back to when people had to pay a toll to use a turnpike (main) road, so the Sparepenny Lane was cheaper than the main route. Come and explore the route of the River Darent, running through the village, flowing under a nineteenth century, red brick railway viaduct, passing a 'Roman villa', a 'castle' before meandering off. Lullingstone Park has a history tracing back at least two thousand years, when the first settlers cleared the woodland to cultivate the soil.

The Romans had a strong impact in the area with many people farming for export. Iron Age farmsteads were abandoned but this is now a major Roman site in Britain. It was first excavated in 1949, once the area around had been cleared, as it was used as a dummy airfield in the Second World War. (Opening times summer 9am to 5pm Monday to Saturday. 10am to 5pm Sundays. Winter (January/February) Wednesday to Saturday 9am to 4pm. 10am to 4pm Sundays.) Built in the first century AD and occupied by several families, the bathhouse, exquisite mosaic flooring, and the system of underfloor heating are all preserved and worth a visit. Look out for a small dog print, embedded in a tile, which had just been made. A free audio tour gives a glimpse of middle class life. Lullingstone 'castle' is not really a castle but a large family estate, with documented evidence that the park was once a vast estate with a deer park, for the gentry to hunt deer and rabbit, with a manor house built in the 15th century. Between the gate and the house stands the ancient church of St Botolph, known as The Church on the Lawn. The house was restored in the eighteenth century in honour of Queen Anne who often visited. In the 1870s Sir William Hart Dyke and two friends framed the rules for lawn tennis, playing the first game there. Lady Hart Dyke started a world famous silk farm in part of the house providing silk for Queen Elizabeth's Coronation robes in 1937 as well as the two princesses Elizabeth and Mary Rose. During World War Two it went to make parachutes.

Coming up to date, the castle now boasts a World Garden of Plants in the grounds where over 10,000 species of plant from all corners of the world can be seen. House open April to October: Friday, Saturday 12noon-5pm. Sunday 2-6pm. Bank Holidays. Admission charge. In the grounds of the park a good percentage of the trees date from when the park was first enclosed as a deer park five to six hundred years ago. It also boasts of having one of the largest collections of 'pollarded' trees in the south east. (Pollard tree: has been managed in the way of having its branches cut to a height beyond the reach of browsing animals, so providing shade and shelter, but still allowing the owner to harvest timber). The Lower Beechen Wood along with Home Wood, have Beech and Sweet Chestnut, Hornbeam, Hazel and Oak coppice trees which have encouraged woodland plants to thrive when the canopy is open to let light through. Woodland Hawthorn and Crab Apple as well as Wood Sorrel and Butcher's-broom have all thrived in the ancient wood. Upper Beechen Wood has more pollarded trees of Oak and Hornbeam, with the Hornbeam being a speciality of the park.

Old and Bold Explored (Lullingstone Walk 1)

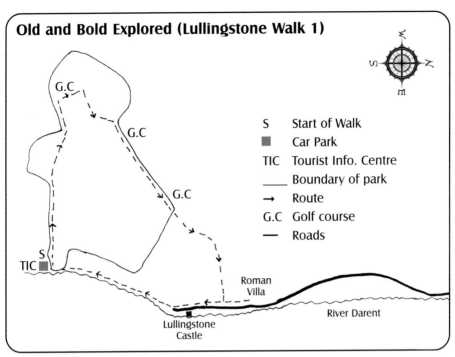

S   Start of Walk
    Car Park
TIC   Tourist Info. Centre
____ Boundary of park
→   Route
G.C   Golf course
—   Roads

Old and Bold Explored (Lullingstone Walk 2)

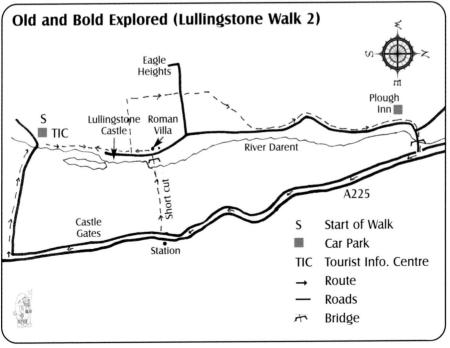

S   Start of Walk
    Car Park
TIC   Tourist Info. Centre
→   Route
—   Roads
⌒   Bridge

Access/parking: Go through Eynsford village on the A225 from the A20. Pass Eynsford station and stay on the road. Going uphill bear right into Castle Road (narrow road). At the bottom turn right into the car park.

Map reference: OS Explorer 147. GR527638

Distance: Walk 1. 4^1/$_2$ miles. Walk 2. 5miles (*) Short cut 4^1/$_2$miles

Time: Walk 1. 2+ hours. Walk 2. 2^1/$_2$ hours (*) Short cut 2hours

Terrain: Walk 1. Steep climb up, grass paths, mud paths, cutting over sections of golf course, road walking. Walk 2. Road walking, mud paths, field walking.

Refreshments: Tourist Information Centre April-September 10am-5pm daily. October-March 10am-4pm daily. Parking £1 all day. Hot and cold meals served. The Plough Inn, Eynsford. Hot food served midday. Roman Villa small selection of drinks, snacks available.

Extra in Area: Eagle Heights, a bird of prey centre with Owls, Condors, Eagles, Vultures, as well as snakes, iguanas, and other reptiles. Flying spectaculars twice daily March-October, once daily November to February. Indoor demonstrations. Open daily 10.30am-5pm March-October. Weekends only 11am-4pm November to February. Tearoom and toilets. Admission fee.

Route Direction

WALK 1 Once parked head for the gate at the back of the car park, go through onto a grass path walking round then heading uphill past fencing on the left. Coming to the top corner go through a gate walking up a steep mud path heading into Lower Beechen Wood. Once at the top bear left and stay on the mud path as it winds round, going straight on at the next junction heading now into Home Wood walking through Sweet Chestnut, Hazel and Hornbeam coppice. As the path goes down, and then up, look out for the iron fencing on the left which is the remnants of the deer fencing enclosure. Once on the flat continue on to the junction, passing farm buildings, and go on 20 yards; stay on the path as it heads

Lullingstone Castle.

downhill. At the bottom the path crosses the golf course (take care crossing, check for golfers in area); go straight over into the woods up a steep short slope coming out onto a lush green expanse of grassland. Head straight on to a concrete pathway and turn right walking along the path heading for woods. Turn left at the gate and enter the woods on a mud path. Take second right onto a mud path as it winds through the woods with the golf course visible through the trees. Coming out of the woods bear left with the path as it cuts across a grass field to the opposite corner.

Stay on the path going downhill, with wooden steps aiding the descent, to the bottom where bushes hide the golf course over to the right. Climbing up again pass pollarded trees on the right. Staying on the flat on a grass path cross a field and head for the line of trees ahead, go through the gap and turn right. Now on a thin mud path continue going downhill on an uneven, rugged path to steps. Go down the steps, through the gate and turn right (turn left walking 200 yards to the Roman Villa site and return to gate) walking on a concrete road. Stay on the road passing houses on the right, then fields on the left.

Pathway beside River Darent, Walks 1 and 2.

Continue on past the stables, coming to Lullingstone Castle on the left. Passing the castle go through the gate ahead onto a concrete/mud path walking beside the River Darent. Stay on the path as it winds with the contour of the river, to a gate and a wooden obelisk on the right, then turn up the pathway into the car park.

WALK 2 From the car park walk past the Tourist Information Centre and bear right going through a gate and down a slope to a wooden obelisk; turn left staying on the concrete/mud path, walking beside the River Darent. Go through a gate onto a tarmac road with Lullingstone Castle on the right. Carry straight on passing fields on the right, then houses on the left before turning the corner. Just on the bend stay on the left side of the road and turn left onto a mud path leading up into woods. Go through the gate, up the steps and continue uphill on the thin winding rugged path. Reaching the flat at a junction turn right heading into a field. Stay on the path at it crosses a second field, coming to a tarmac road. Cross over the road onto a mud path opposite, heading downhill through more fields.

At the bottom cross over the railway line, turn left going down onto the road and turn

Ancient viaduct on Walk 2.

left again. Continue along the road going under the ancient viaduct and coming to low lying fields where highland cattle graze. Continue walking with the contour of the River Darent to open grassland beside the river. (Over on the left a watering hole, The Plough Inn, is tempting on a hot summer's day). Continue round, going over the hump bridge and stay on the right. On reaching the main road turn right. Stay on the pavement passing a few shops before heading out of the village. As the path slowly climbs Eynsford railway station appears on the left. Coming onto a grass verge continue along the road passing the gatehouse of Lullingstone (take care, traffic can be busy). Still slowly climbing take the next turn on the right walking down the narrow road, (care with traffic). At the bottom of the hill bear right going up the drive into the car park.

(*) **SHORT CUT.** Coming up to the station on the left look out for a gate, and a grass path on the right. Go down the path walking between fields of crops before fields where horses are exercised. Carry on past the stable block staying on the grass/mud path to a cattle grate and bridge. Cross over walking past a car park, the Roman Villa straight ahead, turn left walking along the concrete road, passing houses and on past Lullingstone Castle, through the gate and following the route of the River Darent back to the obelisk where turn right up into the car park.

Mighty oak.

Hilltop Rise Walk (Farningham)

This ancient woodland of 168 acres situated on a small hill is 125 metres at its highest point above sea level. The diverse soils including Thanet Sands, Woolwich and Blackheath beds with the majority being Upper chalk, allow a wide range of plant life to thrive. The area has been designated a Site of Special Scientific Interest and a Nature Reserve. Heather and Lily of the Valley grow higher up with Birch, Oak, Hornbeam and Sweet Chestnut trees thriving throughout the woods. Beech, Hazel and Cherry trees are found on the lower slopes along with Spurge Laurel, and Yellow Archangel. The Small-leaved Lime found here and one other site in Kent (Clowes Wood) indicates that the area is ancient woodland, managed for the wood content, but has never been cleared. Along the southern boundary another rare plant the Deptford pink thrives in the summer months. The hedgerows encourage many species of butterfly like the

Meadow Brown and Gatekeeper along with the Holly Blue which feeds on the many Holly trees in the woods and many Woodpeckers, Tree creepers, and Nuthatch along with Warblers frequent the woods in the summer.

Pathway on return walk.

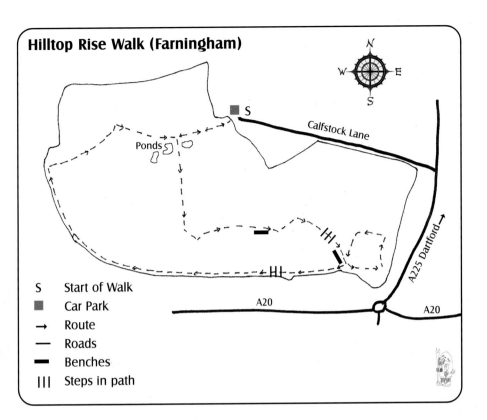

Hilltop Rise Walk (Farningham)

S   Start of Walk
■   Car Park
→   Route
—   Roads
▬   Benches
||| Steps in path

Calfstock Lane

Ponds

A225 Dartford →

A20

A20

Access/Parking: From the A20 head towards Farningham. Take the A225 towards Dartford. Take the second turn on the left into Calfstock Lane, go along the single track road all the way to the end. Free car park.

Map Reference: OS Explorer 162. GR543684

Distance: 4 miles.

Time: 90 minutes +

Terrain: Mud paths, gravel paths, steps in paths, steep up and down.

Refreshments: No toilet facilities in car park. Petrol garage for drinks, snacks on roundabout with A20, A225 interchange, ½ mile from Calfstock Lane turning.

Route Directions

Walk to the back of the car park and go through the wooden posts onto a stone/mud path. Stay on the path as it climbs passing Holly and Chestnut trees onto the flat top; over to the left are the first of three ponds, which are often no more than dry dips. Go through the gate now seeing the other two ponds on the right. These areas are very relevant to the natural ecosystem of the woodland, providing water for the many species of animal and bird found in the area. Stay on the mud path as it winds ignoring any side turnings, walking through a versatile woodland, with wide open rides each side of the path. At the fork, bear left going downhill to a main junction, where go straight on passing a log bench seat on the right, and start to climb. Passing an ancient tree on the right the path starts to descend with steps hewn into the path to aid descent. At the bottom go through the gate and down two steps, then turn left heading into dense woodland. Stay on the mud path as it meanders then descends slightly. Bear round with the path and turn left passing fencing on the right, which is protecting the fields set aside by the Countryside Stewardship Scheme for natural management of land.

These areas have no fertiliser or herbicides so wild rarer flowers are returning like the St Johns Wort, Common Centaury and Common Spotted Orchid. (Dogs must be controlled in the area of sheep grazing). The view from this point is of the viaduct in Eynsford, with the background of the Downs. Bear left with the path climbing up through coppice trees onto a wider mud path on the flat. A welcome bench ahead affords more views of the Downs. From the bench walk straight ahead to the fencing then turn right heading uphill. Stay on the path as it levels out for a short distance, passing paths off to the right before steps once again aid the ascent. Bear round with

Fencing created from woods on return path.

Ponds at start of walk.

the path out into the open with fencing on the left protecting crop fields and the woods on the right. Again ignore the paths off to the right, slowly descending with a corridor of trees ahead, passing coppice Chestnut that has aided the creation of a fenced hedgerow along the path. Go into the corridor of Chestnut, on the mud path, now in a much darker environment than before, still going down. Coming to a stone path on the right, turn right heading uphill on a steep winding path walking between Beech, Chestnut, and Holly with brambles creeping onto the path. Once at the top go through the gate and turn right. Stay on the mud/stone path climbing up onto the flat, with the ponds on the right. Stay on the path as it descends slowly back down into the car park.

Ranscombe Reserve (Near Strood)

This area of 560 acres is a jewel in the crown of the North Downs escarpment, nestling within rolling hills, allowing all to explore a classic landscape that has not greatly altered since the eighteenth century. Woodlands, arable fields and chalk grassland allow a rich diversity of wildlife to flourish in the midst of a working farm. A Dene hole, estimated to have been created in the 1400s has been unearthed by a tractor wheel. This area will be excavated and covered by a grille, which will encourage bats to find homes within the chambers of the hole. Lots of wildlife live in the reserve including badgers, foxes, rabbits and dormice. A recent survey has found that the dormouse is slowly coming back after a sharp decline over the whole country.

Further over to the west the Mausoleum, built in 1783 for the third Earl of Darnley, was once a magnificent building of Portland stone with red marble facings and Doric columns. Although sadly neglected it still holds its own in the annals of important buildings in Kent. It is now being restored to its former glory. Cobham Wood, incorporating the West Kent Downs Countryside Trust, is an area of 165 acres of wood pasture within the boundary of Cobham Park. It has been given a Site of Special Scientific Interest status due to the areas of chalk grassland, coppice and secondary woodland that have been set aside to allow Birch, Pine, Sycamore, Sweet Chestnut and scrub species like Dogwood and Blackthorn to flourish. These encourage birds such as the Nightjar, Nightingale, Woodpecker, Sparrow Hawk and Kestrel. Foxes, adders, rabbits, and Common lizard can be spotted in the area which is also known for its rare orchids and Broad-leaved Cudweed and Hairy Mallow.

A special addition to this walk is Cobham village. The Leather Bottle Inn is where Dickens visited on many occasions and still has associations. The Ship Inn, as the story goes, was built up from timbers from a shipwreck. The thirteenth century church of St Mary Magdalene claims to have more brasses than any other church in England, and the Darnley Arms, possibly of twelfth century origin, has a tunnel connecting it to the church perhaps used by smugglers as an escape route in hard times. There is also the story of a Darnley heir, the Hon. Ivo Bligh who occupies a unique position in cricket. In 1882 England lost the Ashes to Australia for the first time. Like many cricket enthusiasts Ivo was upset and being a cricketer himself took a party over to Australia to win back the Ashes. Whilst there his future wife presented a pottery urn to Ivo, the England captain, with the ashes of a cricket ball inside. After Ivo's death his wife presented the urn to the MCC where it stays on show, despite whoever wins the series.

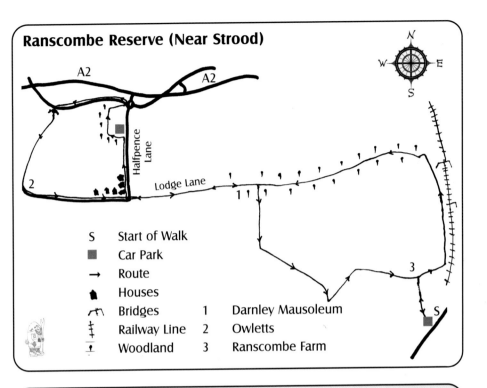

Ranscombe Reserve (Near Strood)

S	Start of Walk
■	Car Park
→	Route
♠	Houses
⌒	Bridges
‡	Railway Line
↑	Woodland

1	Darnley Mausoleum
2	Owletts
3	Ranscombe Farm

Access/parking: From the M2 turn off onto the A228. At the first roundabout go straight over. At the next roundabout take the second turning heading for Cuxton. Go along 50 yards, turn right into the car park.

Map reference: OS Explorer 163. GR718674

Distance: 11 miles

Time: 4+ hours with stops.

Terrain: Grass slopes, grass/mud paths, steps, field walking. Mud paths can be slippery after rain and in winter. Road walking.

Refreshments: Leather Bottle pub in Cobham village. Café on main road.

Route direction

From the car park walk up the concrete path onto the flat and carry on to the junction just before the farmhouse. Turn right walking over crop fields on a thin mud path heading downhill towards the railway line and woods. Go through the woods coming out into a grass area with a railway bridge ahead, turn left by the post just before the bridge, onto a grass path heading uphill. Continue going up on a mud path walking beside the main railway line on the right and woods on the left, passing a bridge on the right. Continue climbing to a second bridge where wooden posts line the path on the right. Turn left just 20 yards ahead on a wide mud path into woodland. Continue on the path as it twists and turns round fallen trees, and as it starts to climb the path turns to gravel/mud. On reaching the top ignore the paths off to the left and right and continue on to a fenced area, going through the gate into the woods. Coming to a gate and a fenced area go through staying on the wide path to the Darnley Mausoleum.

After going round the mausoleum return to the main path and continue on heading into woodland. Stay on the path coming out into open fields seeing a gate directly ahead. Go through onto a gravel/mud track passing a thatched house on the left. Stay on the path passing houses and fields out onto Halfpence Lane. Turn right, cross over the road walking along the pathway, then continue along the side of the road. TAKE CARE WITH TRAFFIC. Pass an orchard on the left, then coming to a car park on the left, go in. Walk to the back and go through the gate onto a wide mud path heading uphill. At the junction turn right onto a grass path which winds round to the larger of the two ponds, where in the summer months the stunning pink of Rosebay Willowherb can be seen. Continue on up heading into dense woodland. At the junction turn right and continue on out of the woods; stay on the concrete path as it winds round and go through the gate onto the road. Turn left walking alongside the road and bear left heading along a winding road between the main road and railway line. (Take care) Coming to a bend head for the bridge on the left, go over and carry straight on through wooden posts, heading into woodland on a wide stone path. Stay on the path as it descends. Ignoring a path off to the left, continue downhill to a coppiced Chestnut area.

Through the tree line a field is visible ahead with this coppice being used as a rail boundary fence and privet bushes planted to create hedgerows. Walk uphill along the tarmac path onto the flat, where wooden stiles form junctions left and right. Go straight on heading down, then up, passing a yard and pond and continue on past a house on the right to the road. Turn left walking into the pebbled yard of Owletts.

After a quick drink (if open) continue along the main road heading into the village of Cobham. Walk through the village, absorbing all the historic features, to the junction and the war memorial; turn left and go on 50 yards to the next small roundabout, cross over and head up the lane beside the field. (Lodge Lane). Walking along the gravel/mud path pass fields then houses to the thatched house on the right. Go through the gate ahead and stay on the concrete path as it heads into woodland. Continue on the same path as earlier back to the Darnley Mausoleum, on the right. Go straight on, ignore the next junction on the right, and then coming to the wide grass path, turn right walking downhill on a stone/mud path and bear round ignoring the left junction onto the flat. Heading through trees start to climb up then turn left at the gap in the woods, heading downhill on a mud path through the middle of a crop field. At the junction turn left heading downhill through crops on a mud path to the entrance to a tunnel of trees out to more fields. Follow the path down through the crops to the junction near the telegraph poles, now turn left heading uphill going around the edge of the field. Stay on the path climbing up onto the flat, go through a swing gate and stay on the path as it winds through an arch of trees before passing the farm on the left to the concrete road. Turn right, staying on the flat, then downhill back to the car park.

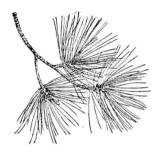

Segment of the Downs Divulged (Holly Hill)

Holly Hill is an area of outstanding natural beauty nestling in the North Downs. A section of the walk before reaching Luddesdown has the name Gag Plantation (gag or gog is an old English name for a boggy place) that refers to the ridge path along the top, as it can be very sticky owing to the clay. Coming into Hatch Hill from the ridge path, this area was used by villagers in the Middle Ages to graze pigs on the beechnuts and acorns on the hilltop as Beech and Oak trees were protected at that time.

Luddesdown Court along with the Church of St Peter and St Paul represent medieval buildings still in use with many features that include a minstrels' gallery in the Court and a fourteenth century tower with corner stones of tufa adorning the church.

Access/Parking: From the A227 head through Vigo Village then towards Harvel. Turn left at a main junction going along White Horse Road then left up Holly Hill. Car park ¹/₂ mile along the road, on the left.

Map Reference: OS Explorer 163. GR670629

Distance: Short walk 3 miles. Long walk 7 miles. (short cut 6 miles)

Time: Short walk 1¹/₂ hours. Long walk 3+ hours.

Terrain: Short walk: mud paths, uneven paths through woods, road walking, stiles, steep climb. Paths through woods can be boggy in summer. Long walk: mud paths, uneven paths through woods, stiles, steep climbs, road walking. Paths through woods can be boggy in summer.

Refreshments: Picnic benches on site of car park. No toilets.

Segment of the Downs Divulged

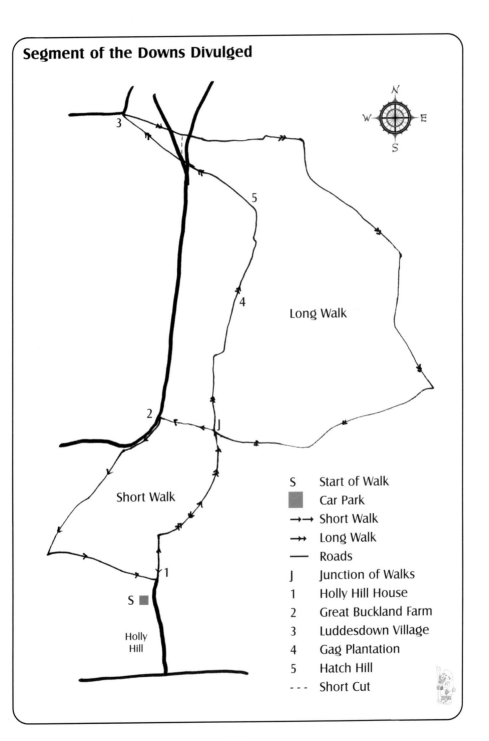

3 Luddesdown Village

5 Hatch Hill

4 Gag Plantation

Long Walk

2 Great Buckland Farm

J Junction of Walks

Short Walk

1 Holly Hill House

S Holly Hill

S	Start of Walk
	Car Park
→→	Short Walk
→→	Long Walk
—	Roads
J	Junction of Walks
1	Holly Hill House
2	Great Buckland Farm
3	Luddesdown Village
4	Gag Plantation
5	Hatch Hill
- - -	Short Cut

Route directions
SHORT WALK. LONG WALK.

From the car park walk down the slope to the road and turn left towards Holly Hill House on the right. Continue along the road passing derelict buildings on the right to a junction heading into woodland. Bear right walking through iron posts, onto a wide mud path as it meanders through the woods of Beech, Ash, Maple and Rhododendron before descending to flat ground towards a junction.

SHORT WALK TURN LEFT. LONG WALK CONTINUE STRAIGHT ON.

SHORT WALK. TURN LEFT Go down the steep mud/stone path to concrete steps and pass by a house on the left as the path descends onto a road track. Cross over and continue straight on, walking on a mud path between houses to the road. Turn left walking along the road ignoring steps and path on right and continue uphill to the junction. Turn left walking into Tranquil Woods Trust land on a grass/mud path. Go through the gate opposite and uphill on a grass path walking past apple trees. Climb over the stile onto a mud path to the next stile. Go over onto a mud/grass path with fencing each side and stay on the path as it winds and climbs, bearing right then left, with breathtaking views across the North Downs all around. Coming onto the flat stay on the mud path as it heads back into deeper woods, climbing again, to a grass area with Cobnut trees on the right. Once on the top go across the open field to the opposite side, then turn left going steeply downhill, cross the road going back uphill directly opposite. Stay on the path to the road. Turn right walking along the road past Holly Hill House then turn right going up into the car park.

LONG WALK. CARRY STRAIGHT ON along the wide flat mud path through the Gag Plantation, meandering through Oak, Beech and Chestnut trees then on past Cedar trees, before coming out into the open. Follow the path round to pylons on the left, then bear right with the path with pylons now on the right. Turn left at the junction onto a mud/stone path, still on the flat, walking through Chestnut and Silver Birch woods. Go straight on at the junction bearing round with the path, (ignore left turn into the field) and continue on as it slowly descends. **(SHORT CUT)** Coming out onto the road bear left, cross over and head into crop fields on a narrow mud path. At the junction carry straight on into Luddesdown village, where the war memorial, church and village hall all represent times past. Walk back along the road to the junction. Go straight on across crop fields to a road, cross over, go through the gap in the hedge into another crop field to a gap in the hedge again. Go through and cross the road going up the steps to the stile.

Short Cut. Coming out onto the road turn right and go straight on for about half a mile to a gap in the fencing on the left, and steps leading up on the right. Turn right up the steps and over the stile onto the Downs. Head straight up the steep hill to the top. The view of Luddesdown village in the valley and the Downs for miles around is worth the climb. The walk will then take you on a mud path, heading uphill into Chestnut coppice woods. Go straight on over the wide grass path, back onto a thin mud path, through more dense woods going downhill. Turn right on a wide grass path heading back uphill into woods. Go round a tree in the path to a junction and go straight on. Turn right at the next junction and bear right onto a wide grass/mud path heading slowly uphill, then bear left heading into deeper woods onto the flat.

Stay on the path as it starts to descend, bearing round (ignore left turn going down) passing Firs on the left as it slowly climbs again. Coming round on the grass path head downhill to the junction. Go straight over uphill on a mud/stone path, bearing left near the top onto a wide mud path, walking through an open tree line. Go straight on a stone path (marked public footpath) past the next junction, now walking on a thin mud path through thick trees to the top of the slope. Turn left, 20 yards on, turn right walking around the edge of a field, then head straight on across an open crop field to the stump in the middle. (North Downs Way) Turn right going up the slope through the fields heading for the woods opposite. Stay on the stone path as it winds through the woods and go through the gate ahead, over the stile opposite and cross the field on the mud path to the opposite corner. Go through the fence into the woods staying on the mud path to a road track. Cross over the stile, bear right going down, then left going uphill across the field, with pylons on the right, heading for the corner at the top. Go through the metal fencing gate and continue straight on (back at junction where short and long walks split), walking on a wide mud path, back through the woods and bear left at the iron gate onto the road. Pass the derelict buildings and Holly Hill House as the path slowly climbs then bear right into the car park.

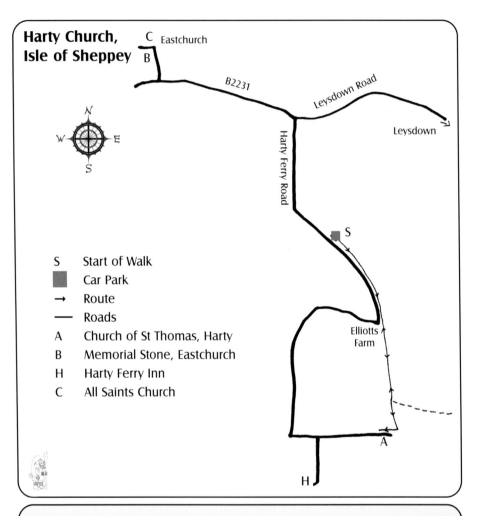

Harty Church, Isle of Sheppey

Legend:
- **S** Start of Walk
- ▪ Car Park
- → Route
- — Roads
- **A** Church of St Thomas, Harty
- **B** Memorial Stone, Eastchurch
- **H** Harty Ferry Inn
- **C** All Saints Church

Map labels: Eastchurch, B2231, Leysdown Road, Leysdown, Harty Ferry Road, Elliotts Farm

---

Access/Parking: Take the A249 road heading north onto the Isle of Sheppey then turn off right onto the B2231 towards Leysdown. After approx.. 5 miles turn right heading for Harty Ferry. Go along the road, using bays as passing points, to a car park on the left.

Map Reference: OS Explorer 149. GR010690

Distance: 4 miles

Time: 2 hours

Terrain: Mud paths, grass paths. Road walking. If not returning by car route, watch out for cars on blind spots.

Refreshments: None en route. Detour to Harty Ferry Inn. Open all day. Hot and cold meals served 12-2pm. Evenings.

Harty Church, Isle of Sheppey

The Isle of Sheppey, ten miles long, five miles wide, was once an island of fertile soil with grazed pastures reclaimed from the Swale River. The Isle of Sheppey (means The Island of Sheep) has villages dotted over the island with historical stories to tell. Include the 2,300 acres of grazing farmland and salt-marsh of a National Nature Reserve and the story never ends; grassland and pools attract wildlife and birds all year round. From the new Kingsferry Bridge onto the island, follow the directions of the Elmley Marshes walk, coming onto the track that winds through the many hundreds of acres of grassland, with pools and ditches which create the Elmley Nature Reserve, home to the Black-tailed Godwit, Snipe and Avocet, while outside the sea wall salt-marsh and inter-tidal mud create valuable feeding grounds for waterfowl including Widgeon, Teal, along with waders like Dunlin and White Plover.

Elmley, once a thriving village at the end of the last century, lying northwest of Kings Hill Farm, with its own school, church, and ferry to the mainland, has disappeared leaving a stretch of deserted shore. The village of Eastchurch was the home of British aviation and moved on from being an eccentric sport to the major industry of today. A memorial of Portland stone in the village, flat on one face and curved on the other, carved with tiny planes depicting the name and year built, is a testament to the pilots who gave their lives, who first flew from the tiny airfield at Stone Pett Farm.

The famous Aero Club of Great Britain founded by the Short Brothers in Leysdown-on-Sea moved to Eastchurch where they bought four thousand acres of land and built the first aircraft factory before moving to Rochester, leaving no trace of the airfield or buildings. Opposite, All Saints Church stands tall and sound, a good example of symmetrical architecture. Built in 1432 to replace an earlier building, the church contains many items of interest and is open daily during the year until dusk. A glass window in memory of the earliest fatal flying accident, when Charles Stewart Ross and Cecil Stanley Grace died in 1910, can be seen.

East of Eastchurch lie the ruins of Shurland, a Tudor mansion with a grim legend attached. Sir Robert de Shurland killed a priest after he had defied his word, and then went to Edward I for forgiveness. On his return from the King's ship Sir Robert met a witch on the shore who foretold his horse Grey Dolphin would one day be the death of him. Sir Robert slew the horse on the beach thinking "I have cheated death once, this horse will not be the death of me". Years later Sir Robert was on the same beach and stumbled over the skull of Grey Dolphin, cutting his toe and contracting fatal blood poisoning. The horse's head appears on the tomb of Sir Robert as a warning against ingratitude.

The Minster area of Sheppey showed to be the highest point on the island, so settlers built their first dwellings. The Abbey Gatehouse and Church are all that remain. It was in about AD670 that a Saxon-widowed Kentish queen, Sexburga, built a monastery becoming its abbess, where royal or noble widows or spinsters could go to rest or retire. As prophesied, Saxon settlers were conquered by the Vikings some two hundred years later. At first the Vikings came to plunder, but they found the 'island of sheep' so welcoming that they stayed and set up their own headquarters for their advance towards the west, remaining masters of the island until the Normans came to conquer. In the early twentieth century property speculators treated Sheppey as a blank cheque

All Saints Church, Eastchurch.

to get rich on. One man, Fredrick Ramus, turned his attentions to the island after doing very well elsewhere. He bought approx. one thousand acres of land, laid out roads and drains and divided the area into plots, on which buyers could build their own homes. He sold three thousand plots to Londoners who believed that Minster-on-Sea could become the nearest health resort to London. Even after the Second World War people wanted a home only as an investment to sell on, not to live in. Today the area is caravan sites and chalets. The furthest end of the island has one of the county's most important nature reserves, the Swale Reserve, where one section is a complete beach of shells, alongside a large area of salt-marsh and a larger area of undrained grazing marsh, forming a wetland extravaganza.

Inland, a reserve has been created where birds of prey like the Marsh Harrier are now beginning to thrive once again, due to the change in farming incentives and the wetland areas, which had been drained, now being restored. The changes have also allowed wildlife like foxes, mice and rabbits to return to their habitats and wild flowers to flourish by the roadside, encouraging butterflies. A whole new ecosystem has returned.

The Isle of Harty, a lonely open spread of land to the south of the island, has its own tale to tell. Harty was until 1610 known as an isle within the Isles of Sheppey. Now it has

All Saints Church, Eastchurch.

St. Thomas's Church, Harty.

its own claim to fame, The Church of St Thomas, a Norman period church which is lit by oil lamps and candles and still has services on the first Sunday of each month. A census in 1891 recorded 125 people living in the village and surrounding area, by 1921 it was 96. People moved away, the school closed, but the church and the Ferry House still remain. The Ferry House Inn was the lifeline of the people of the island as the ferry was owned and run by the landlord, (this still holds today) and was the only means of reaching the mainland of Kent before roads and bridges were built. Many asked why was the church there? Coming in from the sea, merchant ships and men o' war would pass its door on every tide. In times of trouble Harty was a strategic point, with its views down the north Kent coast, and out into the Thames, warnings could be sent over to the mainland. Schooners, barges and oyster smacks traded in Harty until the early twentieth century. The poet laureate Sir John Betjeman said "Alas I shall have to console myself with memories of the church in its splendid isolation, with seabirds wheeling by, the Thames so wide as to be open sea, and air so fresh as to be so healthy" when he had to miss a harvest festival service.

Before reaching Leysdown on the main road a sign on the right indicates CHURCH, HARTY FERRY INN. CAR OR WALK TO HARTY CHURCH. Turn right and follow the road round to a bend. Turn into the car park on the left where the mound allows fantastic views across the marshes of the birds of prey like the Barn Owl and Kestrel all year, Hobby in the summer, Merlin, Short-eared Owl and Peregrine in winter and especially the Marsh Harrier. In the spring the Harriers can be seen gliding across the landscape performing a sky dance. Summer sees the chicks arrive with the male finding food and passing it on to the female in midair for her to then feed the chicks. Autumn sees the arrival of the Scandinavian and east European harriers escaping from the freezing weather. Winter sees the birds flying and resting together in communal roosts.

St. Thomas' Church interior, Harty.

WALK: From the cark park, stay on the road, coming to the junction with Elliotts farm. Turn left onto a concrete road, walking in front of a wooden fence covering a corridor of trees. Stay on the path as it comes to a junction. Ignore the left turn going down the path 200 yards and turn right onto a grass path. Stay on the path as it winds round to a concrete / stone path. Continue straight on downhill passing a junction on the left. Harty church can be seen in the distance over to the right. Stay on the path passing crop fields left and right, where pheasants roam freely and can be seen en masse in the autumn. Bear round to the right to the church.

RETURN: Either, retrace the route back up past the crop fields, up the hill and round. OR take the route of the car completing a circular route.

DRIVE: Turn right and follow the road along as it winds, at the junction turn right. Stay on the road bearing left at the next junction. Where the road bears right going downhill, go straight on into a farmyard, go through onto a dirt road and Harty church is on the right.

Plane on memorial, Eastchurch.

Memorial to British Aviation, Eastchurch.

Elmley Marshes Nature Reserve (Isle of Sheppey)

Elmley and Spitend Marshes are part of the 3,100 acres of land and coastal grazing in southeast England. Wildfowl and waders like Dunlins, Grey Plover and Black-tailed Godwits are seen in great numbers in the winter, while the grazed land is essential for many breeding birds like Yellow Wagtail, Lapwing, Redshank and Avocet in the summer months. Many miles of ditches cross the marshes where dragonflies, water voles and marsh frogs can be spotted, as well as stoats on waste ground. Where there is wildfowl there will also be raptors and this reserve is a good site to see the Marsh Harrier which has colonised the area with many pairs along with Peregrine Falcons, Merlins and Short-eared Owls that often fly in daylight hours.

BINOCULARS ARE A MUST ON THIS WALK TO APPRECIATE THE WILDLIFE.

NO DOGS ALLOWED ON RESERVE.

FROM ENTERING RESERVE YOU ARE REQUESTED TO STAY IN THE CAR UNTIL REACHING THE CAR PARK.

WILDLIFE CAN BE SEEN ALL ALONG THE ROUTE THROUGH THE MARSH LAND.

Path leading back to car park, Elmley Marshes.

Elmley Marshes Nature Reserve

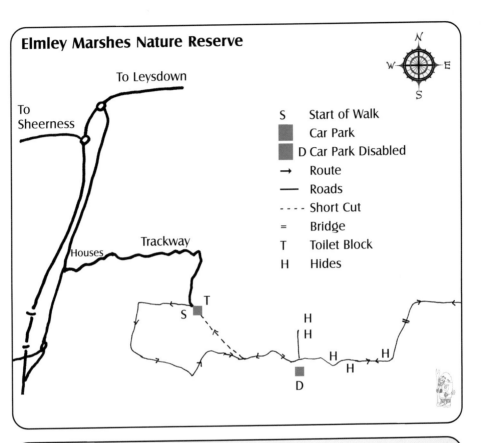

Access/Parking: On the A249 towards Sheerness. Go over the new bridge onto the island. At the first roundabout go right to next roundabout. Go round roundabout taking the second left that comes down the side of the bridge road. Turn left, then left at the houses, and continue on for 3 miles across the open grassland to the farm and car park. NOTE: The reserve is closed on Tuesdays. Free parking. Admission charge. Toilet block only.

Map Reference: OS Explorer 149. GR938678

Distance: 12 miles

Time: 4 Hours+

Terrain: Flat concrete paths, grass paths. Benches on route.

Refreshments: None on site. Nearest town Sheerness 3 miles.

Route directions

From the car park go back to the entrance gate and turn left heading towards a house on the left. Pass the house coming to a gate, go through onto a grass/concrete flat path, passing fencing on the left and trees on the right. Continue on to a derelict house and outhouse on the right. Go through a gate and continue downhill bearing round with the path. Go through the next gate to a junction and another gate. Go round the gate and bear left onto a grass path seeing water channels on the left. Stay on the path at it bears left with views of The Swale ahead and the cement works over to the right. At the seawall bear left with the path walking on the ridge then take the first right following the contour of the ridge on a wide grass path. Coming to the concrete path, bear right, the sea wall forms a high barrier on the right. Stay on the path as it winds round following the contour of the seawall with large pools over to the right and come up to a ridge with open grassland ahead; bird hides are down the path and over to the left along the grass path. Turn right going onto a concrete area for disabled parking, then onto a grass track walking around the edge of the seawall, passing a path on the left going to another three bird hides. Go past a large pool of water on the left then take the path leading off to the left heading into the marsh area to a bird hide at Spitend Point. Turn right and continue along the path walking through the central marshland. Cross the bridge with Dutchman's Island on the right to Windmill Creek. Bear right with the path walking alongside the creek watching for wildlife. Go through the two gates ahead and come up a slope to another path. Return by same path, walking beside the creek to Dutchman's Island, then take the path round to the left following the contour of the seawall, with the salt-marsh area on the left, to Spitend Point. Stay on the seawall path back to the pool now on the right, and continue along the path back up the hill to the car park.

View across the marsh.

Pool en route into Elmley Marshes.

Shellness Adventure (Isle of Sheppey)

(LEYSDOWN, ISLE OF SHEPPEY) Leysdown is the furthest point of the Sheppey island before it comes round creating The Swale waterway. The Shellness hamlet has been cultivated and created as a Site of Special Scientific Interest. Along with The Swale Nature Reserve the area is a haven for nature buffs and an area for exploration for all. The grassland area is predominantly made up of Sea Couch, Marsh Foxtail and Common Bent grasses. Several acres are cut short to allow games to be played while the uncut grasses support a wide variety of insects, including the Meadow Grasshopper, while the Skylarks and Meadow Pipit use the area for nesting. Wild Carrot, Bird's-foot Trefoil, Spear Thistle and the Hoary Ragwort flowers all attract butterflies during the summer months like the Red Admiral, Peacock, Small White and the Gatekeeper.

The beach has its own character being very exposed to both the wind and tides. At low tide shore crabs can be found in the rock pools, birds like the Oystercatcher, Redshank, Dunlin and Knot can be seen feeding on the exposed mud. One section of the beach is a mass of shells aptly called Shellbeach. Thousands of Periwinkle, Cockle, Limpet, Mussel, Whelk and others can be seen all together. The ponds are home to the Emperor Dragonfly and the slender-bodied Damsel Fly in the summer months where they collect around the Common Reed, along with the Marsh frogs. There are no fish in the ponds but the Smooth Newt attaches its eggs to submerged vegetation. Swale Nature Reserve is predominantly salt-marsh on the outer edge with shallow pools at low tide, allowing birds to seek food in the mud. Sea Lavender and Golden Samphire colour the area in summer with brilliant mauve and yellow.

On the inner edge behind the boundary wall, reed beds dominate stretches of the waterways and Canada Geese, ducks, coots along with waders can be spotted. Winter

Access/Parking: From the A249 drive through to Leysdown on the B2231. Carry straight on through the town passing caravan parks. Pass the country park green on the left. Go along the road 1 mile. Car park on left by building.

Map Reference: OS Explorer 149. GR045696

Distance: Short walk 7 miles. Long walk 9 miles.

Time: Short walk 3^1/$_2$ hours. Long walk 4+ hours

Terrain: Flat ground, grass paths, concrete paths. Can be muddy after rain.

Refreshments: Café open 9am-5pm Sat/Sun summer in car park. Cold drinks, snacks available. Toilet block in car park. Leysdown village 2 miles.

Note: In the winter months the car park is closed. Parking is available along the seafront wall, ^{1}/$_2$ mile back along the road. Walking from this point: continue along the seafront to the car park and continue on as directed.

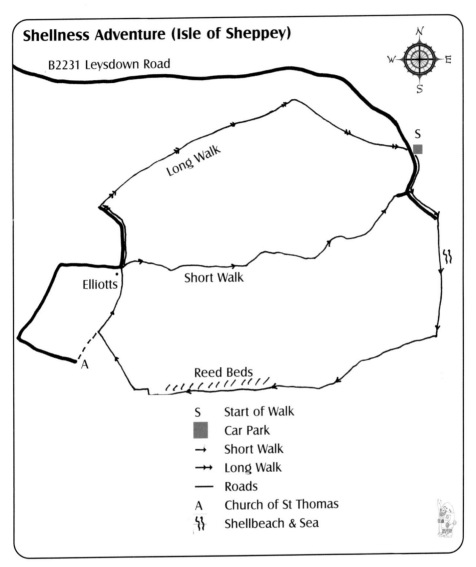

Shellness Adventure (Isle of Sheppey)

B2231 Leysdown Road

Long Walk

S

Elliotts

Short Walk

A

Reed Beds

S	Start of Walk
■	Car Park
→	Short Walk
→→	Long Walk
—	Roads
A	Church of St Thomas
⑂⑂	Shellbeach & Sea

is the best time to appreciate the Reserve for its bird colony as it is home to many Brent Geese, Shore Larks and Snow Buntings along with others. Harty church, its spire heralding the area of Harty, dates from Norman times, and was dedicated to St Thomas. Having low walls topped by a tile roof one side which very nearly reaches the ground. The church is believed to be the most remote in Kent. Being without electricity it is oil lit when the monthly services take place. It also has an intricately carved fifteenth century Flanders kist (chest) dredged up from the Swale, which is now micro-chipped and kept behind a locked area, as it was stolen from the church but retrieved. Within the church stained-glass windows depict both the island, the church, a representation of St Thomas and other scenes.

The historical masterpiece of Saxon and Norman origins is a must to visit either by being incorporated into a walk on the island or by car.

Route directions

Standing in the car park head towards the gate going up onto the seawall. Stay on the seawall path, or come down onto the unmade road running parallel with the seawall heading towards houses in the distance. *If on the unmade road the path comes into a car park, walk over to the far corner going up steps, through a gate, turn right onto a grass ridge path. If on the seawall path, come to a gate, go through then turn right onto the grass ridge path, go through the gate and continue on the grass path.

Continue along the grass ridge with salt-marsh over to the left. Stay on the path as it winds through salt-marsh with pools on the right now much larger and continue on, passing a path down to a lake on the right, to thick reed beds. Follow the path as it passes a bird hide and continues to wind round the contour of the bay. As the path ends in the sheep-wash area, there is a vivid display of open water, fencing and grass over to the right, with the salt-marsh continuing out to the left. Go through the gate still walking on a grass ridge, round to the next gate then cross over the field to the opposite corner. At the top another gate leads onto a gravel path with a line of Hazel trees on the left that breaks up crop fields each side. At the junction turn left onto a road, go along for 500 yards to the church. Once visited return by the same path to the junction, carry straight on going up a slight slope passing a white house on the right.

Stay on the concrete road walking up through Elliott Farm to the road.

Short Cut. Turn right walking on a concrete road heading towards Brewers Hill Farm. Coming to paddock fencing bear left and continue on the path as it winds round, ignoring all side turns. Go straight on at the next junction, with crops either side of the path, and a ditch running alongside on the right. Coming to the next junction bear

Marshland and lakes, Sheppey.

slightly left going up a slope to a gate. Go through heading for a farm and go through the farmyard on a gravel road, bear left then right by caravans to a road. Go left along the road passing a grass area on the right. Coming to a small path cut through the grass and turn right heading into the car park.

LONG WALK. Go straight on, walking along Harty Ferry Road till the road curves to the left and look for the raised raptor viewing point on the right. Just past the viewing point, go through a gate onto a grass path to an enclosed pumping station where turn right. Stay on the path as it winds and twists with the contour of the water for about a mile and a quarter. As the water bears round to the right go through the fenced double gate on the left,

Bird hide on walk.

bear left and cross to a footbridge spanning a ditch. Once over go straight on up the field heading for a fenced corner and continue on, keeping the fence to the left, crossing another field. Go through a metal kissing gate and turn right walking along a grass path to the Country Park. Turn right walking along the road then go up onto the seawall and back to the car park.

Pathway down to St. Thomas' Church, Harty.

Sheep wash-area marshland, Sheppey.

Hucking Heritage (Near Maidstone)

Hucking estate, consisting of woodland, grassland and farmland is spread over 232 hectares on a plateau on the North Downs. Variations in the soil allow for a vast variety of wild flowers and butterflies to flourish along pathways between woodland areas. The quaint village of Hucking, with its tiny St Margaret's church dating back to the Norman period and its pub, the Hook and Hatchet, providing refreshments, lies on an ancient pathway connecting the Downs to Hollingbourne village, its larger protector in times past.

St. Margaret's Church, Hucking.

View across open fields at start of walk.

Hucking Heritage (Near Maidstone)

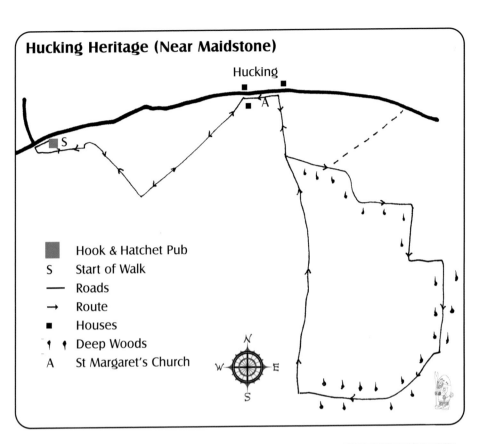

Hucking

A St Margaret's Church

Legend:
- Hook & Hatchet Pub
- **S** Start of Walk
- — Roads
- → Route
- ■ Houses
- ❦ ❦ Deep Woods
- **A** St Margaret's Church

Access/parking: From the A249 towards Maidstone turn left at the sign for Hucking. Climb the hill coming onto a single-track road with passing points. Bear right at the junction, left at the next junction, coming to a T-junction. Turn left, pub car park 50 yards along the road.

Map reference: OS Explorer 148. GR837582

Distance: 2½ miles.

Time: 1½ hours.

Terrain: Grass paths, mud paths, road walking, gravel path. Climbing. Many gates.

Refreshments: Hook and Hatchet pub. Open all day. Meals available in the daytime, Monday to Saturday. Sundays - lunchtime only. Children's play area at back, with picnic benches.

Route directions

From the car park, walk back up the road past the Hook and Hatchet pub to the corner. Turn left into the field. Stay on the left-hand side of the field walking beside fencing, on a short grass path to a gate between trees. Go through the gate into an open field, bear right walking round the edge to another gate. Go through onto a long grass path walkway to the next gate. Once through go straight ahead downhill on open fields covered with Bird's-foot Trefoil, Red and White Heather, Oxeye Daisies and Buttercups. Go past pylons and back up the other side heading for the top left-hand corner walking up beside wire fencing to another gate. Go through onto mud/gravel path and continue up through woods onto a road. Bear right and continue up onto the flat. Stay on the road as it bends round passing a granary and then a house on the right to St Margaret's church before heading down the gravel path beside the churchyard. Go down to the junction then turn left onto a grass path.

Stay on the path to another junction; turn right, going through a gate and into a field, towards the woods. Take the left fork, heading away from the fencing by the woods to a junction where turn right going down to a gate. Go through onto a deep grass path with a vast variety of wild flowers. Turn left at the corner walking beside woodland going uphill and at the next junction turn right into the woods on a grass/mud path. Carry straight on ignoring paths off to the left and right, now going downhill passing six-foot high Rosebay Willowherb plants on the left. At the bottom turn right, go through the gate and cross over the path through the gate opposite. Start to climb up walking on a grass/mud path and ignore a path off to the left before heading downhill. Go through the gate with Cherry trees on the right.

Walking through nature's wonder.

At the bottom go through the gate, turn right, go straight on walking near to the fence out into the middle of open fields. Go straight on, climbing uphill, to another gate. Go through and continue on the grass path walking uphill, staying round the edge of the field by woodland to another gate. Go through onto a concrete path. Turn left heading back to the road and St Margaret's church. Pass the church and continue round the corner, down the hill, bearing off to the left into woods on a mud path. Go through the gate and downhill passing pylons and back up the opposite side to the gate. Go through into the long grass passage to another gate. Go through, turn left, follow the path round the edge of the field to the gate in the opposite corner. Go through, turn right going downhill, walking beside fencing to

'Butterfly Haven' path, Hucking walk.

the gate at the bottom to the Hook and Hatchet pub and just further on the car park.

A Playground For All (Jeskyns Farm) Cobham

Jeskyns Farm is 360 acres of woodland, meadows and orchards bordering Ashenbank Wood. The area has been created from farmland and chalk pits that were used as dumps up until 2006. In the year to its official opening Jeskyns has been transformed into a wildlife extravaganza.

The three main features also have small and large figure sculptures, sculpture seats created from ancient trees, as well as benches all around. Then there is the Hop Pole Dodge, where children dodge between the poles. The Cone Pool where walls have been set up and the pool is no-man's-land is where you have to try to get the cones into your opponent's area, some feat. The Sand Assault Course is great for letting off steam. The Tree House is a marvel; children and adults can climb into the house erected around a fallen tree and see the magnificent views across the park.

Access/parking: Ashenbank car park: From the A2 towards London from Rochester take the Shorne turn off. At the roundabout go straight over heading towards Cobham on Halfpence Lane. Go down ½ mile and the free car park is on the right. **Bridge parking:** From the A2 towards London take the Shorne turn off. At the roundabout take the third turning off going down a slip road by the railway. At the bottom turn left going up a slope over the bridge. Park carefully on the left. **Car Park parking:** Head for Cobham village and go through onto Jeskyns Road then turn right into Henhurst Road. Car park ½ mile on the right.

Map reference: OS Explorer 163. GR678694. **Bridge parking** GR675697. **Car Parking** GR662699.

Distance: Ashenbank car park Walk 1 - 9 miles. **Bridge parking** Walk 2 - 5 miles. **Car park** Walk 3 - 4 miles.

Time: Ashenbank car park Walk 1 - 4+ hours. **Bridge parking** Walk 2 - 2+ hours. **Car park** Walk 3 - 2+ hours.

Terrain: Ashenbank car park: Mud paths, grass paths, road walking, stiles, hills, field walking, flat walking. **Bridge parking:** Mud paths, flat walking, hills. **Car park:** flat walking.

Refreshments: Cobham village ½ mile from car park start. Petrol garage on the A2, one mile towards London for Bridge parking, and Ashenbank car park.

NOTES: The time spent in the park on/at each of the play areas can build into a day's outing for all the family, ideally with a packed lunch. All the paths in the park are accessible for wheelchairs/pushchairs/bikes. Please note that only the CAR PARK parking will be a suitable start for the above.

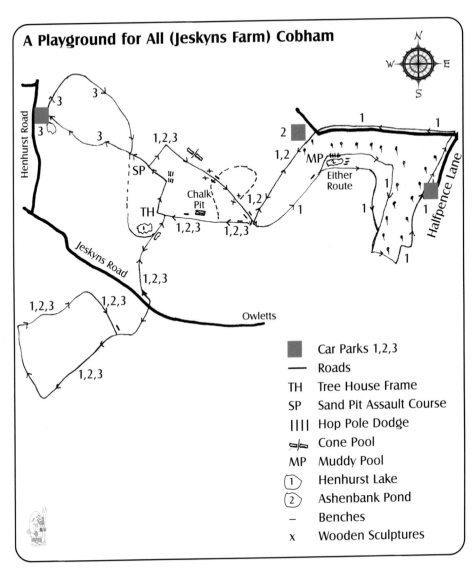

A Playground for All (Jeskyns Farm) Cobham

Legend:

- ■ Car Parks 1,2,3
- — Roads
- TH Tree House Frame
- SP Sand Pit Assault Course
- |||| Hop Pole Dodge
- ⧈ Cone Pool
- MP Muddy Pool
- ① Henhurst Lake
- ② Ashenbank Pond
- – Benches
- x Wooden Sculptures

The Meadows cover approx. 148 acres of land within the park making it one of the largest expanses of wildflower-rich areas in Kent. The grasses include Common Bent, Meadow Barley, Quaking Grass, Red Fescue, Sedge, Tall Fescue, Yorkshire Fog and Upright Broom. Flowers include Bird's-foot Trefoil, Bulbous Buttercup, Common Sorrel, Goatsbeard, Oxeye Daisy, Red Clover, Salad Burnet, Pepper Saxifrage, Meadow Buttercup, Lady's Bedstraw, Cowslip, Chicory, Cornflower, and Red Shank. These encourage birds like the Meadow Pipit and Skylark and butterflies like the Common Blue, Gatekeeper, Marbled White and Meadow Brown to the area. Orchards in Kent have declined over the last fifty years, the 2-mile Orchard walk within the park is a

Ashenbank lake.

feature that has seen over one thousand trees planted to create an area where Apple, Pear, Plum, Cherry, Walnut and Cobnut trees will bring back part of the history of Kent in its fruit.

In the pre-Victorian period, orchards were planted on country estates as a status symbol for the nobility, with varieties like Harvey, Golden Pippin, London Pippin, Golden Bounty and Scarlet Croften. By the Victorian period everyone wanted to grow fruit, but the transportation and distribution proved difficult, so many more varieties were added to the local areas.

Coming up to date, most orchards have changed from the open tall trees, to the small closely planted variety for maximum crop. In supermarkets it's the traditional apple on sale. Over the years an array of apples have been grown, which have been linked to either local people or places like Pippin, Aromatic Russet, Withington, Fillbasket and Maidstone Favourite. These types are being grown in the orchard along with the Cobnut. A Cobnut is a type of Hazelnut introduced in the nineteenth century. Children used to play an early form of conkers with hazelnuts called 'cobnut' and the winning nut was 'the cob'. There are more Cobnut trees in Kent than in any other county. The woodland area to the north of the park bordering Ashenbank is a designated Site of Special Scientific Interest.

Careful management will create, over time, a more dense woodland in the park with seedlings creating the mighty Oak and deadwood providing the habitat for insects and fungi. Henhurst Lake and a smaller pond near by have been created to provide a habitat for many varieties of wildlife, including the endangered Great Crested Newt, Frogs, Toads, Dragonflies, Damselflies, Water Boatmen, as well as providing a drinking and bathing area for the many birds nesting nearby like the Coot, Mallard and Moorhen.

Seating and decking has been provided so that all can enjoy the sights and sounds surrounding the pond. Ashenbank Pond to the north of the park nestling in the field by the woodland expanse, is another example of the diverse landscape opened up for wildlife to exploit, and people to watch nature in action. There are also two large chalk pits, one in the orchard area, and one by the tree house. Both are working examples of re-generation from rubbish pits, to areas where plants and animals are being encouraged to re-colonise.

Walk 1 - Starting from Ashenbank Car Park: From the car park walk up
the hill on the concrete/mud path to the junction, turn right walking on a grass mud path which winds through many ancient trees and stumps which are home to a great variety of insects. Stay on the path as the larger of the two ponds comes into view on the left and continue on up into the woods. At the junction turn right and continue on; once out of the woods, stay on the concrete path as it winds round, go through a gate onto the road. Turn left walking along the road and bear left, heading along a winding road, walking between the main road and railway line. (Take care) Coming round a bend, head for the bridge on the left, go over and carry straight on through wooden posts. Head into woodland on a wide mud/stone path. Stay on the path as it descends; ignore a path off to the left and continue going downhill to a coppiced Chestnut area. Walk uphill along the tarmac path onto the flat; wooden gates form a junction each side of the path.

(RIGHT LEADS INTO JESKYNS PARK) Turn right going through the gate, take the left fork heading downhill on the tarmac path to the chalk pit on the right, with a bench nearby. Just up the path on the left is the tree house. Take the left fork just before the tree house and follow the path round to Henhurst pond on the right with a tiny pond on the left. After visiting the pond continue on the tarmac path to the road. Cross over and go through the gate opposite and up the slope onto the flat. Follow the path round to the board which details the newly-planted fruit trees.

Follow the path round the orchard, coming back to the Orchard Sculpture. Stay on the path back to the board, then cross over the road and go through the gate staying on the tarmac path. Pass the small pond on the right with the tree house ahead. At the junction turn left and bear right with the path to the Hop Pole Dodge on the right. At the junction go straight on seeing the sandpit assault course over to the left. At the next junction go left walking on a grass path up to the fixture. Return on the same path and go straight on to the next junction. Turn right coming to the Cone Pool on the left. Carry straight on to the tall figure sculptures and just further on more sculpture seats are positioned. Go through the gate ahead, over the tarmac path, through the gate opposite then directly left onto a tarmac path. Continue going down, staying on the path as it winds round and crosses the field, coming to a small watering hole (MUDDY PIT) on the opposite side near to the chestnut boundary fencing. Stay on the path to the gate, go through and directly opposite is Ashenbank Lake.

EITHER walk behind the platform there heading across and uphill through a field of Cornflower and other plants, towards the woodland boundary. Stay on the path as it edges round the field to an opening on the left, go through the gate and carry straight on (heading uphill). OR go back to the gate, turn right walking slowly uphill to steps on the right. Go up the steps into the woods on a thin mud path. Stay on this path as

Muddy pit area, near Ashenbank pond.

it winds past a magnificent Wild Service Tree on the right at the top of the slope, before going down and round. Coming to a junction bear right onto the main path in the woods, heading downhill passing ancient gnarled Chestnut trees. Bear left **(heading uphill)** on a mud path and on reaching the top turn sharp left still climbing up. Follow the path round to a fallen tree in the path, where a step has been cut out of the trunk. Once over follow the path round the ancient twisted Chestnut tree to four more steps cut into trunks of fallen trees. At the junction turn left going uphill passing Chestnut, Ash and Beech trees before coming onto the flat, still going through woods with an open grass area off to the left. Continue on the path as it winds past many ancient twisted Chestnut trunks covered with burrs and bearing left on the main path, continue through the woods coming out at the junction, turn right heading downhill to the car park at the bottom.

Walk 2 - Start from the Bridge: PARK BESIDE THE ROAD: go through the concrete posts heading into woodland on a wide mud/stone path. Stay on the path as it descends and continue downhill to a coppiced Chestnut area. Then walk uphill along the tarmac path onto the flat where wooden gates form a junction each side of the path.

(RIGHT LEADS INTO JESKYNS PARK) Now follow the directions in Walk 1 to where the sculpture seats are positioned. Then go through the gate ahead, turn left going down the hill and back up through the woods on a wide mud path. At the top the path comes out by the concrete posts near where the car is parked on the bridge.

Walk 3 - Starting from the Car Park in Henhurst Road. Bear left in the car park and follow the path round to a junction, turn left then right to the Cone Pool. Stay on the path to the sculpture seats then the Tall figure sculptures, and more of the sculpture seats. At the top bear left heading downhill on the tarmac path to the chalk pit on the right, with a bench nearby. Just up the path on the left is the tree house. Take the left fork just before the tree house and follow the path round to Henhurst pond on the right with a tiny pond on the left. After visiting the pond continue on the tarmac path to the road. Cross over and go through the gate opposite and up the slope onto the flat. Follow the path round to the board which details the newly-planted fruit trees. Follow the path round the orchard coming back to the Orchard Sculpture. Stay on the path back to the board

Path in Ashenbank Wood.

then cross over the road and go through the gate staying on the tarmac path. Pass the small pond on the right with the tree house ahead. At the junction turn left and bear right with the path to the Hop Pole Dodge on the right. At the junction turn left with the Sandpit Assault Course on the right. Pass through parkland planting and another small lake back into the car park.

New orchard just planted.

Henhurst pond, Jeskyns.

Hop pole dodge, Jeskyns.

Path through orchard walk.

Tree house, Jeskyns Park.

Cone pool, Jeskyns Park.